# Hearty Salads

# Hearty Salads

Maxine Rapoport with Nina Graybill

Farragut Publishing Company
Washington, D.C.

PRINTED IN THE UNITED STATES OF AMERICA

Cover illustration by Judy Barczak

Library of Congress Cataloging-in-Publication Data
Rapoport, Maxine.
    Hearty salads.

    Includes index.
    1. Salads.   I. Graybill, Nina.   II. Title.
TX740.R35     1989     641.8′3     89-11623
ISBN 0-918535-08-5

*To* Victoria, Andy and Adam—finally
M.R.

*To* the chorus line: Nornie, Nancy, Kitty, Ginger,
Genie and Connie
N.G.

# Introduction

*H*earty salads are just what their name implies—substantial salads that take the place of the more usual meat-starch-vegetable main course. Standing alone, or rounded out by the addition of a hot or cold soup as a first course, and perhaps some crusty bread, hearty salads are the answer to today's quest for lighter, nutritious meals that emphasize freshness and variety. While hearty salads are a summer natural, they also provide a refreshing change of pace in the colder months.

These salads tend to stretch a little meat or poultry a long way, making them economical as well as healthful. Well-flavored beans may replace meat altogether, with no loss of protein. And the inventive uses of potatoes, rice and pasta in these salads give us the high-carbohydrate foods recommended by many nutritionists.

As always the ingredients should be the best quality you can afford. Look for unblemished fruits and vegetables, wash them well and let them drain thoroughly before storing. Tomatoes and many fruits should not be refrigerated until flavors develop fully. Should you find yourself with limp carrots or wilted celery, pare and slice as desired, then cover with cold water for about 30 minutes; they'll usually revive quite nicely.

Feel free to substitute ingredients but be aware that using diced carrots, for example, in a recipe that calls for snow peas dramatically changes both taste and texture. On the other hand, using a little more or less of an ingredient won't make that much difference; so simply add the extra half-cup of diced chicken—and a bit more dressing if necessary.

These recipes serve six generously. Plan ahead: roast two chickens instead of one; buy a slightly larger roast than you'll need; make extra rice, pasta or potatoes. A day or two later you can quickly put together a hearty salad and no one will complain, "But we just had chicken. . . ."

Thanks to the many friends who so generously shared their ideas and recipes. We hope you, your family and guests will find these main course salads delicious and satisfying. Enjoy!

# Contents

# Vegetable Salads

# Vegetable Salads

Vegetables, grains and pasta, alone or in combination, tossed in a tasty dressing, answer many of your meal-planning needs. These salads can accompany a grilled steak or roast chicken; provide a light, lower-calorie dinner; or give the vegetarians among your family and friends a satisfying and nutritious meal.

# New World Buckwheat, Sweet Peppers and Feta Cheese Salad

*The method for cooking the buckwheat might be the same that your mother or grandmother used, but this is definitely a salad for today. Buckwheat groats, also called kasha, are really seeds and not of the grain family.*

1-1/2 cups buckwheat groats

1 egg, lightly beaten

4 cups boiling water

1 small onion stuck with 2 whole cloves

1 bay leaf

2 teaspoons salt

2 tablespoons olive oil

1 medium onion, thinly sliced and separated into rings

1 large sweet green pepper, diced

1 large sweet red pepper, diced

4 ounces Feta cheese, crumbled

1/2 cup chopped parsley

1/3 cup olive oil

3 tablespoons red wine vinegar, or more to taste

1 teaspoon oregano, crushed

1/2 teaspoon ground cumin

1/2 teaspoon freshly ground pepper

Salt to taste

*R*inse the buckwheat groats with cold water and drain well. In a medium saucepan, combine the groats with the egg and cook for a few minutes until they separate. Stir in the boiling water, onion, bay leaf and salt; bring to a boil, reduce heat and simmer 5 minutes. Pour into a colander or sieve, rinse with cold water and discard onion and bay leaf; transfer to a large serving bowl and cool to room temperature.

*H*eat 2 tablespoons oil in a skillet and fry onion rings until brown and crisp; set aside.

*I*n a small bowl, whisk together oil, vinegar and seasonings (do not add salt until salad is mixed as the Feta cheese tends to be salty). Pour dressing over groats, add green and red peppers, Feta cheese, onion rings and parsley and gently mix together. Taste for salt and adjust to taste. Serve salad at room temperature or lightly chilled.

*S*erves 6.

# Ida's Original Lentil Salad

*You might like to precede this protein-packed salad with a smooth and tart cold cucumber-yogurt soup.*

2 cups lentils, rinsed and picked over
4 cups water
1 medium onion stuck with 3 whole cloves
1 bay leaf
2 teaspoons salt
1/2 cup olive oil
1/4 cup white wine vinegar
2 garlic cloves, minced
1/2 teaspoon dry mustard
1/2 teaspoon sugar

1/2 teaspoon thyme
1/2 teaspoon ground cumin
1/2 teaspoon Worcestershire sauce
1/2 teaspoon freshly ground black pepper
Salt to taste
1/2 cup chopped green onions
1/4 cup chopped parsley
4 hard-cooked eggs, quartered

Cook the lentils with the water, salt, onion and bay leaf, covered, for 20 minutes or until soft but not mushy. Drain in a colander and remove the onion and bay leaf. Transfer the lentils to a bowl and while hot mix in the dressing. Refrigerate several hours or overnight.

While lentils are cooking, whisk together the oil, vinegar, garlic, dry mustard, sugar, thyme, cumin, Worcestershire and pepper; set aside until lentils are cooked and drained.

Before serving salad, add green onions and parsley and adjust seasonings to taste. Garnish with egg quarters.

Serves 6.

# Jacob's Red Lentil and Rice Salad

*This is a very festive-looking salad and the fresh cilantro and dill give it a fresh, crisp taste. Serve it with crusty Italian bread.*

1 cup red lentils (available in natural food stores)

3 cups water

1 teaspoon salt

1/4 cup olive oil

3 tablespoons white wine vinegar

Salt and pepper to taste

1 cup rice

2 cups water

1 teaspoon salt

2 cups fresh bean sprouts, rinsed and drained

1/2 cup sliced green onions

2 tablespoons minced fresh cilantro or parsley

2 tablespoons snipped fresh dill or 2 teaspoons dried dill

1/2 cup olive oil

1/4 cup white wine vinegar

1/2 teaspoon salt or more to taste

1/2 teaspoon freshly ground pepper

Chopped fresh cilantro and dill, for garnish

Romaine lettuce leaves, for garnish

*I*n a small saucepan, cook the lentils with the 3 cups of water and 1 teaspoon salt, covered, for 20 minutes or until just tender. Drain the lentils in a colander and rinse with cold water to stop the cooking process. Transfer to a large serving bowl and toss with the olive oil, vinegar and salt and pepper to taste. Cook the rice in the remaining 2 cups water and 1 teaspoon salt for 20 minutes. Add to the lentil mixture and set aside to cool.

*W*hisk together the olive oil, vinegar and salt and pepper; set aside.

*W*hen lentil and rice mixture is cool, add the bean sprouts, cilantro, dill and dressing; toss thoroughly but gently. Refrigerate until serving time. Taste for seasoning before serving; garnish with additional chopped cilantro and dill and surround salad with crisp romaine lettuce leaves.

*S*erves 6.

# Lentil and White Bean Salad with Anchovy Croutons

*The white beans create a visual contrast with the dark lentils, as well as add more protein to this healthful and tasty salad. Serve with sliced fresh tomatoes and cucumbers.*

1-1/2 cups lentils, rinsed and picked over
4 cups water
2 teaspoons salt
A bouquet garni of 1 bay leaf, 4 whole cloves, 6 peppercorns, 1 teaspoon thyme, all tied in a square of cheesecloth
2 large carrots, scraped and cut in 1/2 inch dice
1 cup coarsely chopped onion
2 garlic cloves, minced
16-ounce can small white beans, drained
1/2 cup chopped sweet red pepper
1/2 cup oil, half olive and half salad

1/4 cup red wine vinegar, or more to taste
1 teaspoon salt
1/2 teaspoon freshly ground pepper
2 tablespoons capers, drained
1/4 cup chopped cilantro or parsley
6 hard-cooked eggs, quartered
18 anchovy-flavored croutons
*Croutons*
18 slices French bread, cut 1/4 inch thick
2-ounce tin anchovy fillets, drained
1/3 cup olive oil
1 egg yolk

Add lentils, water, salt and bouquet garni to a large saucepan. Cover, bring water to a boil and reduce heat; add diced carrots and simmer for 10 minutes. Add onions and garlic and simmer 10 to 15 additional minutes or until lentils are just tender. Drain in a colander and remove bouquet garni.

Whisk 1/2 cup oil, vinegar, salt and pepper and capers together in a large serving bowl. Add hot lentils and mix gently. Set aside to cool. When lentils are cool, add white beans and red pepper and refrigerate while preparing croutons. The salad can be refrigerated up to 2 days before serving.

Brush French bread slices with part of 1/3 cup olive oil and lightly toast on both sides. Add anchovy fillets and egg yolk to blender or food processor and blend until just mixed. Slowly add remaining olive oil and blend until smooth. Spread one side of each crouton with mixture.

At serving time, transfer the lentil salad to a shallow platter; garnish with anchovy croutons and quartered eggs and sprinkle with chopped cilantro.

Serves 6.

# Snappy Lentil Salad with Deviled Eggs

*Lentils have been a part of man's diet since ancient times. This salad has a tart taste from the capers and a subtle taste of salt from the anchovies.*

1-1/2 cups lentils, rinsed and picked over

5 cups water

2 teaspoons salt

1/2 cup chopped dill pickles

1/2 cup sliced green onions

2-ounce tin anchovies, drained and chopped

3 tablespoons capers, drained

1/4 cup minced parsley

1/2 cup olive oil

1/4 cup white wine vinegar

1/2 teaspoon dillweed

1/2 teaspoon salt

1/4 teaspoon freshly ground pepper

12 deviled egg halves (use your favorite recipe)

Romaine lettuce, to line platter

Add lentils, water and salt to a large saucepan; cover and bring to a boil, reduce heat and simmer 20 minutes. Drain lentils in a colander and cool to room temperature. Transfer to a large bowl and add pickles, onions, anchovies, capers and parsley.

In a small bowl, whisk together oil, vinegar, dillweed, salt and pepper. Pour over salad, mix thoroughly, cover and chill at least 1 hour. Adjust seasoning to taste after chilling.

At serving time, line a platter or shallow bowl with lettuce leaves, spoon salad in the center and arrange deviled egg halves around salad.

Serves 6.

# Minnesota Rice Salad

*The nutty taste and texture of the wild and brown rices are enhanced by the addition of walnut oil and fresh ginger. Good on its own, or as a side dish with grilled steak or chicken.*

3/4 cup wild rice, rinsed and drained 2 times

3/4 cup brown rice

5 cups water

2 teaspoons salt

2 cups broccoli florets, blanched for 2 minutes in simmering, salted water

6 green onions, chopped

1/2 cup toasted pecans, chopped

1/4 cup minced parsley

Grated peel from 1 orange

Grated peel from 1/2 lemon

1/2 cup extra-virgin olive oil

2 tablespoons walnut oil

1/3 cup fresh orange juice

1 tablespoon lemon juice or vinegar

1 teaspoon grated ginger root

1 teaspoon salt

1/4 teaspoon freshly ground pepper, or more to taste

Bring water to a boil in a large saucepan, add salt, wild rice and brown rice, cover, reduce heat and simmer 20 minutes. Stir and simmer an additional 20 minutes, or until cooked through but not mushy. Pour into a sieve to drain and transfer to a large bowl. Add broccoli, onions, parsley and grated orange and lemon peel; toss to mix.

In a small bowl, whisk together olive oil, walnut oil, orange and lemon juice, grated ginger, salt and pepper. Pour over salad, mix thoroughly and let stand at room temperature up to 2 hours to blend flavors. Taste for seasoning and adjust if necessary.

Serve at room temperature or lightly chilled.

Serves 6.

# Family Favorite Rice Salad

*A* *certain family seems to be locked into this salad, for good reasons too. It's easy to prepare, tasty, and leftovers (should you have any) keep well for days. You might want to serve this with a cold vegetable soup and crisp bread sticks.*

4 cups cooked long grain rice (do not use short grain rice; it becomes too soft and sticky)

1/2 cup sliced celery

4 green onions, sliced

1/4 cup chopped parsley

3 hard-cooked eggs, chopped

1/2 cup mayonnaise

1/4 cup sour cream

1/2 teaspoon salt, or to taste

1/4 teaspoon ground pepper

1 tablespoon salad oil

2 tablespoons vinegar

*I*n a large serving bowl, gently mix the rice, celery, onions, parsley and chopped eggs. Mix mayonnaise and remaining dressing ingredients together in a small bowl. Add to rice mixture and mix thoroughly. Cover tightly and refrigerate until well chilled. Taste for seasoning before serving.

*S*erves 6.

# Peruvian Rice Salad

*You won't have to make a trip to the Andes to enjoy this slightly sweet yet tongue-tingling salad. Warmed pita bread can substitute for a more authentic South American bread.*

4 cups cooked long grain rice

1 cup seedless green grapes, halved if large

1/2 cup raisins

1/2 cup slivered almonds, toasted

1 cup chopped parsley

2 teaspoons grated fresh ginger (do not use ground variety)

1 teaspoon cumin

1/4 teaspoon pepper

1/3 to 1/2 cup fresh lemon juice

1 teaspoon sugar

Salt to taste

Lime wedges for garnish

*I*n a large glass serving bowl, combine all the ingredients and mix gently but thoroughly. Adjust seasonings to taste. Serve lightly chilled.

Serves 6.

# Mississippi Rice Salad

*A plate of hot corn bread and a pitcher of golden honey are all you need to make this a down-home taste treat.*

4 cups cooked long-grain rice

2 cups frozen corn kernels, thawed, blanched 1 minute in boiling water and drained

1 medium sweet green pepper, coarsely chopped

2 medium tomatoes, seeded and coarsely chopped

1/2 cup chopped green onions

1/2 cup coarsely chopped salted or dry-roasted peanuts

1/4 teaspoon crushed red pepper flakes

1/2 cup salad oil

3 tablespoons vinegar, or more to taste

1/2 teaspoon sugar

1/2 teaspoon salt

1/4 teaspoon freshly ground pepper

*I*n a large bowl, mix together rice, corn, pepper, tomatoes, onions, peanuts and pepper flakes.

*I*n a small bowl, whisk together oil, vinegar, sugar, salt and pepper. Pour over salad and toss gently. Cover and chill several hours or overnight before serving.

*S*erves 6.

# Zena's Curried Rice and Banana Salad

*A delightful Australian friend served this at many enjoyable parties. We're not sure if it is really from Australia, but it is delicious.*

3 medium bananas, sliced

1 tablespoon lemon juice

4 cups cooked long grain rice, chilled

1/2 cup thinly sliced celery

1/2 cup green grapes, halved

1/4 cup finely chopped salted peanuts, or dry-roasted

1/4 cup finely chopped green onion, tops only

2 tablespoons chopped pimento

1/8 teaspoon Tabasco sauce, or to taste

1/2 cup mayonnaise

2 tablespoons light cream

1 tablespoon lemon

1 teaspoon curry powder, or to taste

1/2 teaspoon dry mustard

1/2 teaspoon salt

1 tablespoon toasted coconut, for garnish

2 tablespoons chopped chutney, for garnish

Crisp greens to line platter or bowl

*P*ut sliced bananas in a large bowl and sprinkle with lemon juice. Add rice, celery, grapes, peanuts, green onion, pimento and Tabasco, toss lightly, cover with plastic wrap and chill until serving time.

*B*efore serving, mix in a small bowl the mayonnaise, cream, lemon juice, curry powder, dry mustard and salt. Add dressing to rice mixture and toss lightly to mix. Transfer to a shallow bowl or platter lined with crisp greens and top with coconut and chutney.

*S*erves 6.

# Crunchy Brown Rice and Cabbage Salad

*This taste-and-texture-packed salad can stand on its own but you might like to add slivers of left-over meat or poultry for variety.*

4 cups cooked brown rice, chilled

1-1/2 cups shredded cabbage

1 cup thinly sliced celery

1/2 cup finely chopped red onion

1/2 cup finely chopped carrots

1/2 cup chopped parsley

1 tablespoon chopped fresh basil or 1 teaspoon dried

Salt and pepper to taste

1/2 cup olive oil

3 tablespoons red wine vinegar

1 tablespoon tomato paste

1 teaspoon prepared mustard

1/2 teaspoon salt

1/4 teaspoon freshly ground black pepper

Cucumber sticks and red or green pepper rings, for garnish

At least two hours before serving, combine rice, cabbage, celery, onion, carrots, parsley, basil and salt and pepper. Mix dressing ingredients in a small bowl, then mix gently but thoroughly with the salad. Mound onto a platter and surround with cucumber and pepper garnish.

Serves 6.

# Couscous Salad Algiers

*C ouscous is a staple of North Africa. Most of us think of couscous as the complete dish composed of slowly cooked vegetables, meat or chicken and steamed couscous.*

1-1/2 cups couscous, quick-cooking type

4 cups water

1 teaspoon salt

Juice of 2 lemons

1/4 cup olive oil

1 teaspoon ground cumin

1/2 teaspoon ground coriander

Seeds from 3 whole cardamom pods, or 1/2 teaspoon ground cardamom

1/2 teaspoon turmeric

1 large green pepper, coarsely chopped

1 large sweet red pepper, coarsely chopped

1 large tomato, seeded and chopped

1/2 cup chopped parsley

1/4 cup chopped fresh mint (do not use dried mint)

6 green onions, sliced

1/2 cup golden raisins, plumped in boiling water for 10 minutes

2 garlic cloves, minced

2 teaspoons grated fresh ginger (do not use ground ginger)

1/2 teaspoon red pepper flakes

Salt to taste

*B* ring the water and salt to a boil in a medium saucepan, add the couscous and stir constantly until water is absorbed. (This will take just a few minutes.) Remove from heat. Add to a large bowl the olive oil, lemon juice, cumin, coriander, cardamom and turmeric, whisk together; then add the couscous and mix to coat the grains.

*A* dd the chopped peppers, tomato, parsley, mint, green onions, raisins, garlic, ginger and red pepper flakes. Mix thoroughly and taste for salt and other seasonings.

*S* erves 6.

# Baba's Couscous Salad

*This salad of both sweet and savory tastes stands on its own, but the addition of left-over chicken or lamb would add another taste treat.*

| | |
|---|---|
| 1-1/2 cups couscous, quick-cooking type | 1 cup thinly sliced celery |
| 4 cups water | 3/4 cup diced carrots |
| 2 tablespoons olive oil | 1/4 cup thinly sliced green onions |
| 1 teaspoon salt | 3 tablespoons olive oil |
| 1 teaspoon grated fresh ginger | 1 tablespoon fresh lemon juice, or to taste |
| 1 teaspoon curry powder | 1/2 teaspoon cinnamon, or more to taste |
| 1/2 teaspoon cardamom | 1/4 teaspoon allspice, or more to taste |
| 1/2 cup chopped dried figs | 1/4 cup toasted sliced almonds, for garnish |
| 1/2 cup raisins | 1/4 cup chopped parsley, for garnish |

In a medium saucepan, bring the water, 2 tablespoons olive oil and salt to a boil; add the couscous and stir constantly until water is absorbed. Remove from the heat. Stir in the ginger, curry powder, cardamom, figs and raisins. Cover and let stand about 10 minutes. Mix in celery, carrots and green onions and set aside until mixture cools to room temperature.

In a small bowl, mix together the remaining 3 tablespoons olive oil, lemon juice, cinnamon and allspice. Transfer the salad to a serving bowl and gently mix in the dressing. Sprinkle with almonds and parsley before serving. Salad can be refrigerated, but bring to room temperature and taste for seasoning before serving.

Serves 6.

# Polish Potato Salad

---
---

*Most potato salads are acclaimed as good, but this one is always termed sensational. What do you think?*

4 large wax-skin potatoes, cooked and diced

1/4 pound green beans, cut in 1-inch pieces and cooked crisp

2 cups sliced carrots, cooked

10-ounce package frozen peas, thawed and boiling water poured over, then well drained

3 large dill pickles, diced

4 hard-cooked eggs, diced

1 tablespoon fresh dillweed, minced, or 1 teaspoon dried

1 teaspoon caraway seeds

1/2 cup mayonnaise

2 teaspoons Dijon-style mustard

1/2 teaspoon salt, or more to taste

1/4 teaspoon freshly ground pepper

*I*n a large bowl, combine the potatoes, green beans, carrots, peas, dill pickles, eggs, dill and caraway seeds.

*M*ix the mayonnaise, mustard, salt and pepper together and add to the salad mixture. Mix thoroughly, cover with plastic wrap and refrigerate several hours or up to 3 days before serving.

*S*erves 6.

# Potato and Green Bean Salad

*You might like to serve a hot or cold tomato-based soup with this easy but satisfying salad.*

5 medium wax-skin potatoes, cooked and diced

1 pound green beans, cut in thirds and cooked in salted water

4 green onions, thinly sliced

1 whole pimento, cut into thin strips

1/3 cup olive or salad oil

3 tablespoons white wine vinegar

1 large garlic clove, minced

1 teaspoon basil

1 teaspoon salt

1/4 teaspoon freshly ground pepper

1/4 cup chopped parsley, for garnish

*I*n a small bowl, whisk together the oil, vinegar, garlic, basil, salt and pepper. Set aside.

*P*repare the vegetables and combine them in a serving bowl. While the potatoes and beans are still warm, add the dressing and mix gently but thoroughly. Cool to room temperature, cover with plastic wrap and refrigerate if not serving immediately. Bring to room temperature and taste for seasonings before serving.

Serves 6.

# New Delhi Potato Salad

*N*ot only are the spices in this salad different from most of the potato salads we are acquainted with, but so is the method of browning both the spices and potatoes for added flavor.

2-1/2 pounds new red potatoes, cooked and cubed (do not peel)

4 tablespoons olive oil

1 teaspoon cumin seeds

1 teaspoon whole mustard seeds

1/2 teaspoon caraway seeds

1 cup coarsely chopped onion

2 garlic cloves, minced

2 teaspoons grated fresh ginger (do not use ground ginger)

1 teaspoon ground coriander

1/2 teaspoon red pepper flakes

Salt to taste

1 cup plain yogurt

1/4 cup chopped cilantro or parsley, for garnish

*H*eat oil in a large skillet until very hot, add cumin, mustard and caraway seeds and cook just until cumin and mustard seeds begin to pop. Lower heat and when pan cools a bit, add onions, garlic, ginger, coriander, pepper flakes and cubed potatoes. Toss gently with a spatula to coat potatoes with oil and spices. Cook just until onion become limp and potatoes slightly golden.

*T*urn into a bowl, season with salt and mix in the yogurt. Cool to room temperature, cover with plastic wrap and refrigerate several hours or overnight.

*T*ransfer to an attractive serving bowl and garnish with cilantro. Serve with an assortment of Indian breads, if available, or warm pita bread.

*S*erves 6.

# Egg Salad in a Puff Bowl

*This all-time favorite salad makes a statement with its own easy-to-prepare Puff Bowl.*

Puff Bowl (see page 21)

12 hard-cooked eggs, coarsely chopped

1 cup thinly sliced celery

6 green onions, chopped

1/2 cup chopped dill pickles

1/4 cup chopped parsley

2/3 cup mayonnaise

2 teaspoons Dijon-style mustard, or more to taste

1 teaspoon Worcestershire sauce

1/2 teaspoon salt, or more to taste

1/4 teaspoon freshly ground pepper

Green pepper rings, for garnish

Thinly sliced iceberg lettuce, to line Puff Bowl

*P*repare Puff Bowl ahead of time.

*I*n a small bowl, mix together mayonnaise, mustard, Worcestershire sauce, salt and pepper.

*I*n a large bowl, gently mix together eggs, celery, onions, pickles and parsley. Add dressing to egg salad, adjust seasoning if necessary; cover and chill several hours.

*T*o serve, place a layer of sliced iceberg lettuce in the bottom of the Puff Bowl, spoon in the egg salad, garnish with pepper rings and slice into wedges.

Serves 6.

# Puff Bowl

1 cup water

5 tablespoons butter or margarine

1 cup flour mixed with 1/4 teaspoon salt and
a pinch of nutmeg

4 eggs, at room temperature

*B*ring water and butter to a boil in a medium saucepan. Add dry ingredients all at once and stir quickly with a wooden spoon. The mixture will soon pull away from the sides of the pan and form a smooth ball. Remove from heat and stir in one egg at a time; mix until fully incorporated before adding the next egg.

*S*pread the mixture into bottom and up sides of a greased 9- or 10-inch springform pan. Bake in preheated 400-degree oven 40 minutes. Turn off oven and quickly prick the puff all over with a toothpick or cake tester. Close oven door and leave puff in oven 10 minutes. Remove to cake rack and cool in pan. Remove sides of springform pan and transfer Puff Bowl to a serving dish.

*P*uff can be baked up to one day ahead, covered loosely with foil and kept at room temperature. Recrisp in a 400-degree oven for a few minutes; cool before filling. Puff can also be wrapped tightly in heavy duty foil and frozen. Thaw uncovered, and proceed as above.

*S*erves 6.

# Composed Vegetable and Baked Cheese Salad

*This is the type of salad the French have been serving for decades, but it's fairly new to America. The arranging demands a bit of last minute-attention but the result is worth it.*

1/2 pound Gruyere cheese, or other firm cheese such as Swiss or Fontina

3/4 cup butter-type cracker crumbs

2 garlic cloves, minced

1-1/2 teaspoons marjoram, crushed

1 teaspoon freshly ground pepper

1 egg, beaten

16-ounce can whole beets, drained and thinly sliced

3 medium carrots, scraped and thinly sliced on the diagonal and blanched 3 minutes in simmering water

3 medium potatoes, boiled, peeled and thinly sliced

1 head romaine lettuce, cut into 1/2-inch wide slices

1 cup torn watercress leaves and small stems, for garnish

Fresh dill sprigs, for garnish

1 cup extra-virgin olive oil

1/3 cup white wine or herb vinegar

2 tablespoons Dijon-style mustard

2 tablespoon minced fresh dillweed, or 2 teaspoons dried

1/2 teaspoon salt, or more to taste

1/4 teaspoon freshly ground pepper

Cut cheese into 12 equal-size fingers or rectangles.

In a flat dish, combine cracker crumbs, garlic, marjoram and pepper. Add beaten egg to another flat dish. Dip cheese fingers first in the egg, then in the crumb mixture. Place on a foil-lined or non-stick baking sheet, cover with plastic wrap and chill.

In a small bowl, whisk together oil, vinegar, mustard, dill, salt and pepper; set aside.

Prepare vegetables early in day, wrap separately and keep at room temperature. Prior to serving, arrange a bed of lettuce on 6 dinner-size plates; compose beets, carrots and potatoes on the lettuce, drizzle with dressing and sprinkle with watercress.

Bake chilled cheese fingers in a preheated 350-degree oven for 15 to 20 minutes, or until cheese is soft. Place 2 pieces of cheese in the center of each plate, garnish with a dill sprig and serve immediately. Pass the remaining dressing separately.

Serves 6.

# Tabbouleh with a Difference

*This salad is just bursting with nutrition and fiber, and it's a taste treat too. Serve with a basket of Herbed Pita Triangles.*

1/2 cup bulgur wheat (available in natural food stores and large supermarkets)

1 cup lentils, rinsed and picked over

4 cups water

1/2 cup vinegar

2 teaspoons salt

1 medium onion, stuck with 3 whole cloves

4 garlic cloves, lightly crushed

1 bay leaf

1/2 teaspoon thyme

1 cup chopped parsley

1/2 cup olive oil

1/4 cup lemon juice, or more to taste

1 tablespoon chopped fresh mint (do not use dried mint)

1/2 teaspoon salt, or more to taste

1/4 teaspoon freshly ground pepper

Romaine lettuce, to line salad bowl

Mint leaves, for garnish

Soak bulgur in cold water to cover by one inch, refrigerated overnight or for at least 2 hours at room temperature. Drain and press to remove as much water as possible. Transfer to a large bowl; cover and refrigerate.

In a medium saucepan, combine lentils, water, vinegar, salt, onion, garlic, bay leaf and thyme. Cover and bring to a boil, reduce heat and simmer about 25 minutes. Drain, discard onion, garlic and bay leaf. Add lentils to the bowl with the bulgur.

In a small bowl, whisk together oil, lemon juice, mint, salt and pepper. Pour over bulgur and lentils, add parsley and mix. Cover and chill at least 1 hour before serving. Salad can be prepared up to 2 days before serving.

To serve, line a salad bowl with romaine lettuce; taste salad for seasoning and adjust if necessary. Spoon into bowl and garnish with mint leaves.

Serves 6.

# Sparkling Red and Green Bulgur Salad

*E*xcellent for buffets because of the inviting color contrasts.

1-1/2 cup bulgur (cracked wheat, available at nutrition stores and large supermarkets)

2 cups broccoli florets, cut into small pieces

1 cup chicken broth

1/4 cup tarragon vinegar, or more to taste

2 teaspoons Dijon-style mustard

2 garlic cloves, minced

1/2 teaspoon tarragon, crushed

1 teaspoon salt

1/4 teaspoon freshly ground pepper

1/2 cup diced sweet red pepper

1/2 cup diced celery (or fennel for a new taste)

1/2 cup thinly sliced green onions

2 tablespoons extra-virgin olive oil

Chopped parsley, for garnish

*I*n a medium saucepan, bring to a boil chicken broth, vinegar, mustard, garlic, tarragon, salt and pepper. Stir in bulgur, cover and remove from heat. After broth is absorbed, mix in broccoli, pepper, celery and onions. Add oil and additional vinegar to taste. Garnish with parsley and serve at room temperature or lightly chilled.

*S*erves 6.

# Fish and Seafood Salads

# Fish and Seafood Salads

*L*ow *in calories, high in flavor and nutrition, hearty fish and seafood salads always add a luxurious note to special dinners for family or guests. Consider starting the meal with a homemade soup or quiche, and finish with a fabulous dessert, for a true four-star event.*

# Steamed Mussels #1

_Scrub mussels thoroughly and cut off "beard." Discard any with opened or cracked shells. Cover with cold water and 1 tablespoon salt. Soak for 20 minutes. Preheat oven to 450 degrees. Arrange the drained mussels in one layer on a baking sheet and steam in oven for 7 to 8 minutes until the shells have opened. Discard any unopened mussels._

# Steamed Mussels #2

_Clean the mussels as in method #1. Place in a heavy kettle or pot with 1/2 cup dry white wine; cover and cook at a high heat for 5 minutes. Leave the cover on for another 5 minutes. Discard any unopened mussels._

# Rice, Shrimp and Artichoke Salad

*This salad is simplicity itself. You might like to start with a cup of cold soup, and serve both soup and salad with your favorite crunchy bread.*

4 cups cooked long-grain rice

1 quart water, seasoned with 2 teaspoons salt, 8 peppercorns, 1 small onion stuck with 2 whole cloves and 1 bay leaf

1 pound small shrimp, shelled

10-ounce package frozen artichoke hearts, cooked according to package directions, cooled and quartered

2/3 cup extra-virgin olive oil

1/3 cup mayonnaise

1/4 cup lemon juice

3 tablespoons minced green onion tops

1-1/2 teaspoons tarragon, crushed

1 teaspoon salt

1/4 teaspoon freshly ground pepper

Boston or bibb lettuce to line bowl

2 tablespoons each minced green onion tops and parsley, for garnish

*I*n a medium saucepan, bring 1 quart water with seasonings to a boil. Reduce heat, add shrimp and simmer barely 3 minutes. Drain and refrigerate to cool quickly.

*I*n a small bowl, mix together oil, mayonnaise, lemon juice, onion tops, tarragon, salt and pepper.

*I*n a large bowl, mix together rice, shrimp, artichokes and dressing. Refrigerate several hours for flavors to blend.

*L*ine an attractive bowl with lettuce leaves. Taste salad for seasoning and adjust if necessary; spoon into the bowl and sprinkle with minced green onions and parsley.

*S*erves 6.

# Hunan Noodle, Shrimp and Vegetable Salad

*Subtly spicy, this salad tastes best when eaten with chopsticks.*

12 ounces Chinese egg noodles or thin spaghetti

1 tablespoon salad oil

1 pound small shrimp, shelled

2 cups fresh bean sprouts, blanched in boiling water for 30 seconds, drained and rinsed with cold water

1 large cucumber, peeled, seeded and cut in 2-inch julienne strips

1 cup coarsely shredded carrot

8 radishes, thinly sliced

1/4 cup salad oil

1/4 cup soy sauce

3 tablespoons rice vinegar or white wine vinegar

1 tablespoon white wine

1 tablespoon sesame oil

2 teaspoons sugar

1 teaspoon ground ginger

1 teaspoon salt

1/2 teaspoon chili oil, or more to taste

3 tablespoons chopped peanuts

3 tablespoons minced cilantro or parsley

Cook egg noodles or spaghetti just until al dente, drain, rinse with cold water and drain again. Transfer to a bowl and mix with 1 tablespoon salad oil; set aside to cool.

Cook shrimp in simmering salted water for barely 3 minutes, drain and set aside to cool.

In a small bowl, whisk together salad oil, soy sauce, vinegar, white wine, sesame oil, sugar, ginger, salt and chili oil.

Transfer the noodles to a large platter and arrange the bean sprouts, cucumbers and carrots on top. Drizzle with half the dressing. Add the shrimp and radishes and pour on the remaining dressing. Garnish with peanuts and cilantro and serve at room temperature or lightly chilled.

Serves 6.

# Shrimp Monte Carlo

*This salad is a real winner!*

1 quart water, seasoned with 2 teaspoons salt, 8 peppercorns, 1 small onion stuck with 2 whole cloves and 1 bay leaf

2 pounds large shrimp, shelled and deveined

1/2 pound green beans, halved and sliced lengthwise in half

1/2 pound mushrooms, thinly sliced and tossed with 2 tablespoons lemon juice to keep them white

4 medium carrots, coarsely grated

2/3 cup heavy cream, whipped until it mounds softly

1/2 cup mayonnaise

1 tablespoon minced fresh dill or 1 teaspoon dried

1 teaspoon salt, or to taste

1/4 teaspoon freshly ground pepper

Red-leafed or Boston lettuce to line plates

1/4 pound country-type paté, cut in julienne strips, for garnish

Fresh dill sprigs, for garnish

*B*ring 1 quart of water and seasonings to a boil; add shrimp and turn off heat. After 5 minutes, drain shrimp and run under cold water, drain again and refrigerate while preparing vegetables and dressing.

*C*ook beans in boiling salted water for barely 3 minutes, drain, run under cold water and drain again. Refrigerate to cool.

*M*ix whipped cream with mayonnaise, dill, salt and pepper.

*I*n a large bowl, combine shrimp, beans, mushrooms, carrots and dressing; taste for seasoning and adjust. Line salad plates with lettuce leaves and divide the salad equally among the plates. Garnish with paté strips and dill sprigs.

Serves 6.

# Sweet and Sour Cabbage and Shrimp Salad

*This is a rather unusual combination but one we think works successfully.*

1 quart water, seasoned with 2 teaspoons pickling spice

6 cups finely shredded cabbage

1-1/2 pounds small shrimp, shelled

2/3 cup vinegar

1/2 cup salad oil

1/2 cup sugar

3 tablespoons flour

1 tablespoon Worcestershire sauce

2 teaspoons dry mustard

1/2 teaspoon salt, or more to taste

1/4 teaspoon freshly ground pepper

1/2 cup mayonnaise

1 cup garlic or herb croutons, for garnish

*B*ring 1 quart of water and seasoning to a boil; add shrimp, remove from heat and let stand for 3 minutes or just until shrimp turn pink. Drain and rinse briefly with cold water to remove any pickling spice. Refrigerate to cool.

*M*ix sugar, flour and mustard in a medium saucepan. Slowly whisk in vinegar, oil, Worcestershire sauce, salt and pepper. Cook over medium heat until mixture thickens. Remove from heat and stir in mayonnaise. Cool to room temperature, stirring occasionally.

*P*ut shredded cabbage into a large bowl and pour half the dressing over it. Refrigerate for several hours. Gently mix the remaining dressing with the shrimp and refrigerate.

*A*t serving time, arrange a bed of cabbage on 6 individual plates and divide the shrimp equally among the plates. Garnish with croutons.

*S*erves 6.

# Palm Beach Shrimp and Grapefruit Salad

*Perfect choice for a "ladies' lunch." Serve with iced tea and homemade rolls.*

1 quart water, seasoned with 2 teaspoons salt, 8 peppercorns and 1 bay leaf

2 pounds medium shrimp, shelled

1 cup thinly sliced celery

1/2 cup minced sweet red pepper

1/4 cup minced green onions

3 tablespoons minced parsley

1 cup mayonnaise

2 tablespoons lemon juice

2 teaspoons grated lemon peel

1/2 teaspoon salt, or more to taste

Milk to thin dressing

3 small pink grapefruits, peeled, white pith removed and divided into segments

24 small cherry tomatoes

Boston or bibb lettuce to line plates

1/3 cup sliced almonds, for garnish

*B*ring 1 quart of water and seasonings to a boil; add shrimp, reduce heat and simmer for 3 minutes. Drain and refrigerate while preparing vegetables and dressing.

*I*n a small bowl, mix mayonnaise, lemon juice, lemon peel and salt.

*W*hen shrimp has cooled, chop into small pieces and mix with celery, pepper, onion, parsley and 2/3 cup dressing. Taste for seasoning and adjust if necessary. Salad can be refrigerated for several hours.

*T*hin remaining dressing with milk to pass at the table.

*A*t serving time, line 6 salad- or dinner-sized plates with lettuce, place a mound of salad on each plate and surround with grapefruit segments and tomatoes. Garnish with almonds.

*S*erves 6.

# Shrimp, Potato and Pea Salad

*The addition of shrimp lifts this potato salad above the usual picnic fare. Serve with a plate of garden-ripe sliced tomatoes and cucumber sticks.*

1 pound small shrimp, shelled and cooked 2 minutes in simmering salted water, drained and cooled

4 medium red or wax-skin potatoes, cooked, peeled and diced

10-ounce package frozen peas, thawed, blanched with boiling water, drained and cooled

3 medium dill pickles, chopped

4 green onions, chopped

1 cup mayonnaise

3 tablespoons lemon juice

1 tablespoon minced fresh dillweed or 1 teaspoon dried

1/2 teaspoon salt, or more to taste

1/4 teaspoon freshly ground pepper, or more to taste

Cornichons or small dill pickles, thinly sliced lengthwise, for garnish

Pimento-stuffed olives, for garnish

*In* a large bowl, combine shrimp, potatoes, peas, pickles and onions. Cover and refrigerate while preparing dressing.

*In* a small bowl, mix together mayonnaise, lemon juice, dillweed, salt and pepper. Add to salad ingredients and mix thoroughly. Refrigerate salad several hours or overnight.

*At* serving time, adjust seasoning, if needed; turn salad into an attractive bowl and garnish with pickles and olives.

*S*erves 6.

# Bayside Shrimp Salad with Fresh Dill Dressing

*The warm dill dressing gives a distinctively different taste to this easy-to-construct salad.*

2 pounds small shrimp, shelled

8 medium celery stalks, cut on the diagonal into 1-inch pieces

1-1/2 quarts water, seasoned with 1 tablespoon salt, 8 peppercorns and 1 bay leaf

1 large carrot, finely chopped

1/2 cup celery leaves, sliced

3 tablespoons white wine vinegar

2 tablespoons Dijon-style mustard

1 tablespoon flour

1 teaspoon sugar

1/2 teaspoon salt

1/2 cup heavy cream

1/2 cup extra-virgin olive oil

1/4 cup minced fresh dill (do not use dried dill)

Boston or bibb lettuce to line salad plates

Thinly sliced red onion rings, for garnish

Fresh dill sprigs, for garnish

*B*ring seasoned water to boil in a saucepan, reduce heat and add shrimp and celery. Simmer about 1 minute, until shrimp turn pink. Drain in a colander and cool to room temperature.

*M*eanwhile, mix together in a small saucepan vinegar, mustard, water, flour, sugar and salt. Set over medium-low heat and stir in heavy cream; cook until mixture becomes slightly thickened. Remove from the heat, stir in dill and whisk in oil. Cover and keep warm while preparing salad.

*I*n a large bowl, combine shrimp and celery with carrots and celery leaves. Line dinner or salad plates with lettuce and divide salad among the plates. Pour warm dressing over shrimp salad and garnish with onion rings and dill sprigs.

*S*erves 6.

# Sauteed Shrimp with Fresh Basil

*Don't even think of preparing this salad with dried basil; it just won't work. Serve with crunchy Italian or French bread to dab up the tasty dressing.*

2 pounds large shrimp, shelled, deveined and butterflied along the inner curve

2/3 cup extra-virgin olive oil

2/3 cup chopped fresh basil leaves (not packed)

2 tablespoons lemon juice

2 tablespoons dry sherry

1 teaspoon salt

1/2 teaspoon crushed red pepper

Shredded iceberg lettuce to line plates

Rings of sweet red pepper, for garnish

*P*our oil into a large skillet and heat over medium-high heat; add shrimp, basil, lemon juice, sherry, salt and pepper flakes. With a wide spatula, toss and turn shrimp just until they turn pink; do not overcook. Transfer to a bowl and cool to room temperature.

*L*ine 6 dinner-size plates with shredded lettuce. Using a slotted spoon, divide the shrimp among the plates; garnish with pepper rings. Taste dressing for seasoning and adjust if necessary; spoon over each salad and serve.

*S*erves 6.

# Shrimp with Cauliflower and Sugar Snap Peas

*This salad is a visual delight with its contrasting colors. You might like to serve this with Dann's Beer Bread or Biscuits.*

1-1/2 pounds medium shrimp, shelled

1 quart boiling water, seasoned with 1 tablespoon pickling spice tied in a cheesecloth square and 2 teaspoons salt

1 medium head cauliflower, stems discarded and florets broken into small pieces

1/4 pound sugar snap peas, ends trimmed, or 1 10-ounce box frozen sugar snap peas, thawed

1 bunch watercress, coarse stems removed

1/3 cup extra-virgin olive oil

1/3 cup walnut oil (available in specialty food stores and large supermarkets)

1/4 cup sherry wine vinegar

3 tablespoons minced parsley

2 tablespoons minced green onions

1 garlic clove, minced

1/2 teaspoon salt, or more to taste

1/4 teaspoon freshly ground pepper, or more to taste

1/2 cup coarsely chopped walnuts, for garnish

*I*n a small bowl, whisk together olive oil, walnut oil, vinegar, parsley, onions, garlic, salt and pepper; set aside.

*A*dd shrimp to boiling water, reduce heat and simmer about 2 minutes. Drain in a colander, remove pickling spice; transfer to a bowl and mix with 1/4 cup dressing. Cover and chill.

*B*lanch cauliflower in boiling salted water for 1 minute. Drain and rinse with cold water to stop cooking. Drain thoroughly, transfer to a bowl and mix with 1/4 cup dressing; cover and chill.

*B*lanch fresh sugar snap peas in boiling salted water for 1 minute. Drain and rinse with cold water and drain again. Transfer to a bowl and mix with 1/4 cup dressing; cover and chill. If using frozen peas, place in a colander and pour boiling water over peas, drain and proceed as above.

*J*ust before serving, toss together in an attractive salad bowl shrimp, cauliflower, sugar snap peas and watercress. Add remaining dressing and garnish with walnuts.

Serves 6.

# Shrimp and Cauliflower Salad with Mustard-Cream Dressing

*The mustard-cream dressing is also delicious served with warm boiled potatoes and crumbled bacon.*

1-1/2 pounds medium shrimp, shelled

1 quart boiling water, seasoned with 2 teaspoons salt, 8 peppercorns, 1 small onion stuck with 2 whole cloves and 1 bay leaf

2/3 cup coarsely shredded cauliflower

1 large sweet red pepper, halved and cut cross-wise into thin strips

1/2 cup mayonnaise

2 tablespoons Dijon-style mustard

1 tablespoon lemon juice

1/2 teaspoon sugar

1/4 cup heavy cream, lightly whipped

Salt to taste

1/4 cup chopped parsley, for garnish

Freshly ground pepper

*A*dd shrimp to boiling water, reduce heat and simmer 2 minutes. Drain, cool, cut into thirds; refrigerate until well chilled.

*I*n a small bowl, mix together mayonnaise, mustard, lemon juice, sugar and whipped cream; add salt to taste.

*C*ombine in a large salad bowl chilled shrimp, cauliflower, and pepper. Mix in dressing, garnish with parsley and several grinds of black pepper.

*S*erves 6.

# Big Sur Shrimp and Fruit Salad

*Fortunately, you needn't go to California to enjoy this salad—the ingredients can be found in any supermarket.*

2 pounds large shrimp, shelled and deveined

1-1/2 quarts water flavored with juice of 1 lemon, 1/2 cup parsley stems and leaves, 4 green onions, chopped, 1 tablespoon salt, 8 peppercorns

2 ripe but firm pears, peeled, cored and sliced into thin wedges

2 oranges, peeled and white pith removed, broken into segments

1 ripe papaya, peeled, pitted and diced (or 1-1/2 cups pineapple chunks)

1/2 cup extra-virgin olive oil

2 tablespoons fresh lemon juice

1 tablespoon fresh orange juice

1 tablespoon honey

Grated peel from 1/2 lemon and 1/2 orange

1/2 teaspoon salt

Boston or bibb lettuce to line plates

4 green onions, minced

1/2 cup chopped dry-roasted peanuts

*I*n a medium saucepan, bring water and flavoring ingredients to a boil; reduce heat and simmer 10 minutes. Pour through a strainer into another saucepan. Return to heat and bring to a boil again; then reduce heat, add shrimp and simmer 3-4 minutes. Drain and refrigerate while preparing fruit and dressing.

*I*n a small bowl, whisk together oil, lemon and orange juice, honey, grated lemon and orange peel and salt. Taste for seasoning and adjust. Add 1/3 cup dressing to shrimp and toss to coat; return shrimp to refrigerator.

*C*ombine in a bowl pears, oranges, papaya or pineapple and remaining dressing. Refrigerate at least 1 hour to marinate fruit.

*J*ust before serving time, line individual plates with lettuce, arrange equal number of shrimp attractively on plates and top with mixed fruit. Sprinkle each plate with minced onions and chopped peanuts.

*S*erves 6.

# El Capitan Shrimp and Avocado Salad

*This salad shows that the current craze for Southwestern foods is completely understandable.*

1-1/2 pounds medium shrimp, cooked in salted water, cooled and diced

2 avocados, peeled, pitted and diced

1 large sweet red pepper, diced

1/2 cup chopped green onion

1/3 cup minced cilantro or parsley

3/4 cup extra-virgin olive oil

1/3 cup lime juice

Grated peel of 1 lime

1/2 teaspoon oregano, crushed

1/2 teaspoon salt, or more to taste

1/2 teaspoon crushed red pepper

Shredded iceberg lettuce, to line salad plates or platter

7-ounce bag taco chips, lightly crushed

18 cherry tomatoes, halved, for garnish

3 hard-cooked eggs, sliced, for garnish

Pitted ripe olives, for garnish

*I*n a small bowl, whisk together oil, lime juice, lime peel, oregano, salt and pepper flakes. Taste for seasoning and adjust if necessary.

*I*n a large bowl, mix together diced shrimp, avocado, pepper, green onions, cilantro and 2/3 cup dressing. Chill for at least 1 hour.

*A*t serving time, line individual plates or a large platter with shredded lettuce, top with crushed taco chips, then add chilled salad. Garnish each plate or platter with tomatoes, sliced eggs and olives. Drizzle with remaining dressing or pass separately.

Serves 6.

# Shrimp with Cellophane Noodles and Cucumbers

*C*ellophane noodles are great fun to cook. If they're not available in your area, substitute extra-thin spaghetti.

1-1/2 pounds small shrimp, shelled, cooked, halved and mixed with 1/3 cup dressing and chilled

7-1/2 ounce package cellophane noodles, cooked according to package directions, drained, mixed with 1/3 cup dressing and chilled

2 medium cucumbers, peeled, seeded and sliced

2 cups sliced Chinese cabbage (bok choy)

6 green onions, sliced into 1-inch pieces

1/2 cup salad oil

1/4 cup rice vinegar or white wine vinegar

1 tablespoon soy sauce

2 teaspoons dry sherry

2 teaspoons sesame oil

1 garlic clove, minced

Salt to taste

1/4 teaspoon freshly ground pepper

1 small sweet red pepper, thinly sliced, for garnish

2 tablespoons toasted sesame seeds, for garnish

*B*efore preparing shrimp and noodles, whisk together in a small bowl oil, vinegar, soy sauce, sesame oil, garlic, salt and pepper. Add to shrimp and noodles as directed above; reserve remainder.

*I*n a large bowl, toss together noodles, shrimp, cucumbers, sliced cabbage, onions and remaining dressing. Taste for seasoning and adjust if necessary. Garnish with pepper strips and sesame seeds.

*S*erves 6.

# Beach-Time Crabmeat and Apple Salad

*Make this easy salad early in the morning, then enjoy the rest of your day without worrying about "what's for dinner."*

1 pound cooked crabmeat, picked over
1 cup diced red-skinned apple (not peeled)
1 cup diced Monterey Jack cheese
1 cup diced hard-cooked eggs
1/2 cup chopped green onion
1/2 cup chopped parsley
1/2 cup olive oil
1/3 cup mayonnaise
2 tablespoons lemon juice
1 tablespoon dry sherry
2 teaspoons Dijon-style mustard
1/2 teaspoon salt, or more to taste
1/4 teaspoon freshly ground pepper
1/2 cup toasted sliced almonds, for garnish

*In* a large bowl, mix together crabmeat, apples, cheese, eggs, onions and parsley; cover and refrigerate while preparing dressing.

*In* a small bowl, whisk together oil, mayonnaise, lemon juice, sherry, mustard, salt and pepper. Taste and adjust seasoning if necessary. Add dressing to salad ingredients, cover and chill at least 2 hours before serving. If possible, serve salad in individual large shells or shell-shaped dishes.

*S*erves 6.

# Crab Salad Hawaii

*A*nother easy but tasty salad that's well-suited to casual summertime dining.

12 ounces cooked lump crabmeat, chilled

1-1/2 cups cooked rice, chilled

1-1/2 cups pineapple chunks, packed in natural juice, drained (reserve 1 tablespoon juice for dressing)

1 cup small seedless green grapes, or larger ones halved

1/2 cup toasted shredded coconut

2/3 cup mayonnaise

1 tablespoon pineapple juice

1 teaspoon grated fresh ginger

Salt to taste

*I*n a large bowl, combine crabmeat, rice, pineapple, grapes and coconut.

*I*n a small bowl, stir together mayonnaise, pineapple juice, ginger and salt to taste. Add to salad ingredients, gently mix. Serve lightly chilled.

*S*erves 6.

# Beaufort Crab Salad

*The coastal waters of the American South abound in crabs. This recipe was designed to take advantage of that bounty.*

1 small head iceberg lettuce, cored and halved and thinly sliced

2 tablespoons extra-virgin olive oil

1 tablespoon lemon juice

1/4 teaspoon salt

1/4 teaspoon thyme

1 pound lump crabmeat, picked over

1 large turnip, peeled, thinly sliced and cut into 2-inch-long julienne strips

1/2 cup diced sweet red pepper

1/4 cup minced green onions

1/2 cup mayonnaise

2 tablespoons lemon juice

1 tablespoon extra-virgin olive oil

1/2 teaspoon salt

1/4 teaspoon freshly ground pepper

4 hard-cooked eggs, quartered, for garnish

*In* a small saucepan, bring 1 cup water to a boil, add julienned turnip and simmer barely 2 minutes. Drain, rinse with cold water, drain again and pat dry. Set aside to cool.

*Toss* sliced lettuce with oil, lemon juice, salt and thyme; place in a large salad bowl.

*In* a small bowl, stir together mayonnaise, lemon juice, oil, salt and pepper.

*In* a bowl, combine crabmeat, turnip, onions, pepper and dressing. Spoon salad on top of the lettuce in the bowl, surround with eggs and sprinkle with dill.

*Serves* 6.

# Scallop Ceviche and Rice Salad

*Scallops "cooked" in lemon juice are combined with well-seasoned rice for a truly tasty salad.*

1 pound bay scallops (or sea scallops, quartered), drained and patted dry with paper toweling

1/4 cup lemon juice

1 tablespoon extra-virgin olive oil

1/2 teaspoon salt, or more to taste

1/4 teaspoon freshly ground pepper

1/2 teaspoon thyme

1 garlic clove, finely minced

3 cups cooked long-grain rice, chilled

3 tomatoes, preferably peeled, seeded, juice squeezed out and pulp coarsely chopped

1 small red onion, halved and thinly sliced

1/4 cup chopped fresh basil (if not available substitute parsley)

1/2 cup extra-virgin olive oil

2 tablespoons white wine vinegar

1 tablespoon raspberry vinegar, or more to taste

1/2 teaspoon salt

1/4 teaspoon freshly ground pepper

*I*n a small bowl, whisk together lemon juice, oil, salt, pepper, thyme and garlic. Place scallops in a glass bowl or plastic bag, pour marinade over, cover or seal and refrigerate overnight. Stir occasionally.

*I*n a large salad bowl, whisk together oil, wine vinegar, raspberry vinegar, salt and pepper. Add rice, tomatoes, onion and basil and mix. Drain scallops (discard marinade) and mix into rice mixture. Taste for seasoning and adjust if necessary.

*S*erves 6.

# Scallops with Greens and Avocados

*Scallops are a nice change from shrimp and make a refreshing summer lunch or dinner.*

2 pounds bay scallops, or sea scallops quartered

1 quart boiling water, seasoned with 2 teaspoons salt, 8 peppercorns and 2 tablespoons lemon juice

2 cups shredded Boston lettuce

1 bunch watercress, coarse stems removed, leaves and remaining stems coarsely chopped

2 Belgian endives, trimmed and sliced in 1/2-inch pieces

1 large red sweet pepper, cut into 1/2-inch dice

2 large tomatoes, seeded and chopped

1/2 cup extra-virgin olive oil

3 tablespoons red wine vinegar

1 tablespoon dry sherry

2 teaspoons sesame oil

2 tablespoons minced fresh basil leaves, or 1 teaspoon dried

2 tablespoons minced green onion tops

1 tablespoon sesame seeds

1 garlic clove, minced

1/2 teaspoon salt, or more to taste

1/4 teaspoon freshly ground pepper

Boston lettuce to line plates

3 avocados, peeled, seeded and sliced (sprinkle with lemon juice to prevent discoloration), for garnish

2/3 cup Herbed Croutons, for garnish

*R*educe heat of boiling water, add scallops and simmer just until they become opaque. Drain, rinse with cold water, then drain thoroughly. Refrigerate until chilled.

*I*n a small bowl, whisk together oil, vinegar, sherry, sesame oil, basil, onion tops, sesame seeds, garlic, salt and pepper.

*C*ombine in a large salad bowl lettuce, watercress, endives, pepper, tomatoes and chilled scallops. Pour dressing over salad, taste for seasoning and adjust if necessary. Line dinner-size plates with whole lettuce leaves, divide salad among the plates and garnish with avocado slices and croutons.

*S*erves 6.

# Curried Mussel, Potato and Pea Salad

*P*otatoes, peas and curry powder are staples of India. The mussels add a French or Italian or American note, making this salad truly international.

3 pounds mussels (see introduction to Seafood Salads for methods for steaming mussels)

2 pounds small new potatoes, scrubbed, cooked and quartered

10-ounce package tiny peas, thawed, blanched with boiling water and drained

4 green onions, minced

*Curry Vinaigrette:*

2/3 cup extra-virgin olive oil

1/4 cup white wine vinegar

1 garlic clove, minced

1 teaspoon curry powder

1/2 teaspoon salt

*Curry Mayonnaise:*

3/4 cup mayonnaise

1 tablespoon extra-virgin olive oil

2 teaspoons Dijon-style mustard

2 teaspoons curry powder, or more to taste

1/2 teaspoon salt

1/4 teaspoon freshly ground pepper

Chopped cilantro or parsley, for garnish

*I*n a small bowl, whisk together oil, vinegar, garlic, curry powder and salt; set aside.

*I*n another small bowl, stir together mayonnaise, oil, mustard, curry powder, salt and pepper. Taste for seasoning, adjust if necessary and set aside.

*S*team mussels, cool just enough to remove mussels from shells; while still warm mix with 1/4 cup Curry Vinaigrette.

*C*ook potatoes until almost soft, drain, transfer to a large bowl and mix with remaining Curry Vinaigrette. Add mussels, blanched peas and onions to the potatoes and mix gently. Add Curry Mayonnaise and mix again. Cover and chill for several hours.

*A*t serving time, transfer the salad to an attractive shallow bowl or platter and sprinkle with cilantro.

*S*erves 6.

# Ponte Verde Mussel Salad

*An unusual spicy salad to perk up jaded taste buds.*

3 pounds mussels (see introduction to Seafood Salads for methods for steaming mussels)

3 cups frozen corn, thawed, blanched with boiling water and drained

1 cup coarsely chopped sweet red pepper

1/2 cup chopped green onion

4-ounce tin chopped chilies, drained

1/4 cup chopped cilantro or parsley

2 garlic cloves, minced

3 tablespoons red wine vinegar

2 tablespoons olive oil

1 teaspoon salt

1/2 cup mayonnaise

1/4 cup bottled chili sauce

1 teaspoon chili powder

1/2 teaspoon salt

4 slices bacon, crisply fried and crumbled, for garnish

3 tablespoons chopped cilantro or parsley, for garnish

Cool steamed mussels, remove from the shell and place in a large ceramic or terra cotta serving bowl. Cover and chill.

Mix together corn, pepper, onion, chilies, cilantro, garlic, vinegar, oil and salt. Cover and let stand at room temperature at least 2 hours.

In a small bowl, mix together mayonnaise, chili sauce, chili powder and salt. Chill until mixed into salad.

One hour before serving, combine corn relish with mussels. Stir in mayonnaise dressing, adjust seasoning if necessary, and return to refrigerator.

At serving time, mix crumbled bacon into salad and sprinkle with cilantro.

Serves 6.

# Mussels and Rotelle with Garlic Sauce

*This salad is definitely for the garlic lover, and if you love mussels and pasta too, more the better.*

3 pounds mussels (see introduction to Seafood Salads for methods for steaming mussels)

1/2 pound rotelle, cooked al dente, drained and tossed with 1 tablespoon olive oil

1 cup thinly sliced celery

1/4 cup chopped green onions

1/4 cup chopped parsley

1/2 teaspoon thyme

1 thick slice Italian or other dense bread

3 tablespoons white wine vinegar

8 garlic cloves, quartered

1 egg yolk

1 tablespoon boiling water

1 tablespoon lemon juice

1/2 teaspoon salt, or more to taste

1/4 teaspoon freshly ground pepper

1 cup extra-virgin olive oil

Salt and pepper to taste

Sliced garden-ripe tomatoes, for garnish

Cool steamed mussels, reserve cooking liquor. Remove mussels from shells and add to a large bowl with cooked pasta, celery, onions, parsley and thyme. Toss together, cover and chill while preparing garlic sauce.

Tear bread into a small bowl, add vinegar and soak for 10 minutes. Squeeze out as much liquid as possible and discard. Add bread and garlic to food processor bowl or blender jar and whirl until very smooth. Add egg yolk and blend. Very slowly, while motor is running, add oil until all is incorporated. Add boiling water and lemon juice very slowly so that sauce remains very thick. Transfer to a bowl and mix in reserved mussel liquor.

Gently stir garlic sauce into mussel and pasta salad. Salad can be garnished with tomatoes and served immediately or refrigerated overnight. Garnish with tomatoes at serving time.

Serves 6.

# Mixed Seafood and Vegetables with Tonnato Sauce

*The classic tuna sauce, used here to dress seafood and vegetables, could also be served with cold sliced veal or turkey breast.*

1-1/2 pounds medium shrimp, shelled
1 pound bay scallops, or sea scallops, sliced
2 cups water
1/2 cup dry white wine
1 stalk celery, with leaves, cut into 1-inch pieces
1 carrot, scraped, cut into 1-inch pieces
1 small onion, stuck with 2 whole cloves
1 bay leaf
8 peppercorns
1 teaspoon salt
1 cup diced zucchini
1 cup diced carrots
1 cup thinly sliced celery

1/4 cup thinly sliced green onions
7-ounce can oil-packed tuna, drained
1/2 cup mayonnaise
2 tablespoons lemon juice
2 tablespoons dry white wine
2 tablespoons capers, drained
2 garlic cloves, sliced
1/2 teaspoon tarragon
Salt to taste
1/4 teaspoon freshly ground pepper
Romaine lettuce, to line platter or bowl
Minced parsley, for garnish

*I*n a medium saucepan, bring to a boil water, wine, celery, carrot, onion, bay leaf, peppercorns and salt. Reduce heat and simmer, uncovered, 10 minutes. Pour through a strainer into another saucepan and reheat to simmer. Add shrimp and cook barely 2 minutes, then remove shrimp with a slotted spoon and refrigerate. Add scallops to simmering bouillon and cook just until opaque, less than 2 minutes. Remove with a slotted spoon and refrigerate. Discard bouillon. Shrimp and scallops can be cooked day before serving. Diced vegetables can also be prepared day before serving, stored tightly wrapped and refrigerated.

*A*dd to food processor bowl or blender jar tuna, mayonnaise, lemon juice, wine, capers, garlic, tarragon, salt and pepper and mix until smooth. Transfer to a container and refrigerate up to 1 day.

*T*o assemble salad, mix seafood, vegetables and tonnato sauce in a large bowl. Taste for seasoning and adjust if necessary. Line platter or bowl with romaine lettuce, mound salad on top and sprinkle with parsley.

Serves 6.

# Carmel Seafood Salad

*Picture-perfect Carmel, California, offers many delights, including this salad. Serve with Parsley Skillet Bread and a California Sauvignon Blanc or Zinfandel Blush.*

3 frozen lobster tails, cooked and meat cut into chunks

1 pound cooked small shrimp

1 quart mussels (see introduction to Seafood Salads for methods for steaming mussels)

1/2 pound green beans, tipped, halved and cooked for 2 minutes in boiling salted water, drained and cooled

2 tablespoons chopped sun-dried tomatoes

2/3 cup extra-virgin olive oil

3 tablespoons white wine vinegar

2 teaspoons Dijon-style mustard

2 garlic cloves, minced

3 tablespoons minced fresh dillweed

1 teaspoon salt

1/4 teaspoon freshly ground pepper

Boston or bibb lettuce to line salad plates

Tomato wedges, for garnish

1/4 cup minced parsley mixed with 1 teaspoon grated lemon peel, for garnish

*I*n a small bowl, whisk together oil, vinegar, mustard, garlic, dill, salt and pepper.

*C*ombine in a large bowl lobster, shrimp, mussels, beans, sun-dried tomatoes and half the dressing. Cover and chill for at least 2 hours before serving. Taste for seasoning and adjust if necessary.

*A*t serving time, arrange 2 or 3 lettuce leaves on each dinner-size plate and divide salad among them. Garnish with tomato wedges, drizzle with remaining dressing and sprinkle with parsley/lemon garnish.

*S*erves 6.

# Shrimp, Scallops and Mushrooms with Shell Pasta

*A*nother *elegant seafood salad that makes a wonderful first or main course dish.*

1 pound small shrimp, shelled and cooked 2 minutes in 2 cups boiling salted water, drained and chilled

1/2 pound bay scallops (or sea scallops, quartered), simmered in 1/2 cup water and 2 tablespoons white wine just until they turn opaque, drained and chilled

1 cup small shells cooked al dente, drained, mixed with 1 tablespoon olive oil and chilled

1 pound small mushrooms, quartered

2-ounce tin anchovy fillets, minced

2 garlic cloves, minced

1/4 teaspoon freshly ground pepper

1/2 cup extra-virgin olive oil

1/4 cup red wine vinegar

1/2 teaspoon fennel seeds

Salt to taste

1/4 cup minced flat leaf parsley (if available) or regular parsley

1/4 cup minced green onion tops

*I*n a small bowl, mash together anchovies, garlic and pepper; whisk in oil, vinegar and fennel seeds; add salt to taste.

*I*n a large bowl, mix together shrimp, scallops, pasta shells, mushrooms and dressing. Chill at least 2 hours. Mix again before serving and adjust seasonings to taste. Sprinkle with chopped parsley and green onion tops.

Serves 6.

# Fish and Shrimp Salad in Puff Bowl

*A*nother *Puff Bowl salad, sure to get raves from start to finish.*

1 Puff Bowl (see page 21)

1 pound firm fish fillets (haddock, snapper, cod or salmon); poached 5 minutes in salted water, chilled and flaked

1 pound small shrimp, shelled

2 cups simmering water, seasoned with 1 teaspoon salt, 6 peppercorns, 1 small onion and 1 small bay leaf

10-ounce box frozen peas and carrots, thawed and blanched with boiling water, drained well

1 small sweet green pepper, chopped

1 small sweet red pepper, chopped

4 green onions, chopped

1/2 cup mayonnaise

2 tablespoons catsup

2 teaspoons horseradish

2 teaspoons lemon juice or vinegar

2 teaspoons chopped fresh dillweed or 1/2 teaspoon dried

Salt and freshly ground pepper to taste

3 hard-cooked eggs, quartered, for garnish

Chopped fresh dill (if available), for garnish

*P*repare Puff Bowl in advance as directed.

*C*ook shrimp in simmering water for 2 minutes, drain and chill.

*I*n a small bowl, mix together mayonnaise, catsup, horseradish, lemon juice, dill, salt and pepper.

*I*n a large bowl, mix gently fish, shrimp, peas and carrots, green and red peppers, onions and dressing. Cover and chill for several hours.

*J*ust before serving, place Puff Bowl on a large round platter. Mix salad and adjust seasoning if necessary. Spoon into Puff Bowl, garnish with eggs and sprinkle with dill. Slice salad and bowl in wedges and serve immediately.

*S*erves 6.

# Isle of Rhodes Seafood Salad

*L*et this salad transport you to sunny Greek isles. An elegant main course, or a first course for 12 of your dearest friends.

1-1/2 pounds squid (cleaned at fish counter)

12 prawns or large shrimp, unshelled

1-1/2 pounds small shrimp, shelled and cooked for 1 minute in simmering, salted water

1 small red onion, thinly sliced

1/4 pound Greek olives, or other cured black olives

1/2 cup chopped parsley

1/2 cup extra-virgin olive oil

1/4 cup lemon juice

1/4 cup white wine vinegar

2 garlic cloves, minced

1 teaspoon oregano, crushed

1/2 teaspoon salt, or more to taste

1/4 teaspoon freshly ground pepper, or more to taste

Boston or bibb lettuce to line platter or salad plates

Minced parsley, for garnish

*C*ook squid in boiling, salted water about 20 minutes, drain. Slice body into 1/4-inch slices and chop tentacles.

*I*n a large skillet, heat oil, add prawns or large shrimp and stir and toss about 4 minutes. Remove from heat, add squid, small shrimp, onion rings, olives, parsley, lemon juice, vinegar, garlic, oregano, salt and pepper. Stir well to incorporate all ingredients. Transfer to a large bowl and cool to room temperature. Cover and chill for several hours.

*A*t serving time, line platter or individual plates with lettuce. Arrange prawns on platter or plates and with a slotted spoon mound remaining salad on platter or plates. Taste dressing for seasoning and adjust if necessary, pour over the salad and garnish with parsley.

*S*erves 6.

# Dieter's Delight Seafood Salad

*Low in calories and fat, but high in flavor appeal.*

1 pound salmon steak, cut into 1/2-inch cubes

1 pound flounder fillet, cut into 1/2-inch cubes

1/2 pound bay scallops, or sea scallops halved and sliced 1/4-inch thick

2 large garlic cloves, quartered

2 green onions, cut into 1-inch pieces

1/2 cup fresh basil leaves (if unavailable add 1/4 cup more parsley and 1 teaspoon dried basil, crushed)

1/4 cup parsley leaves

1/2 teaspoon coriander seeds, or 1 teaspoon ground coriander

2 large tomatoes, seeded and coarsely chopped

Grated peel of 1 lemon

2/3 cup lemon juice

1/4 cup extra-virgin olive oil

1 teaspoon salt

1/4 teaspoon freshly ground pepper, or more to taste

Red leaf lettuce, to line salad bowl or plates

Lemon and tomato wedges, for garnish

*I*n a large bowl, combine salmon, flounder and scallops.

*A*dd to food processor bowl or blender jar garlic, onions, basil, parsley and coriander seeds; whirl until finely minced. Add tomatoes and lemon peel and blend just until incorporated. Scrape into a bowl and stir in lemon juice, oil, salt and pepper. Pour over seafood, cover and marinate overnight, stirring occasionally.

*A*bout 1 hour before serving, remove salad from refrigerator; gently stir, taste for seasoning and adjust if necessary. Line a shallow bowl or 6 salad plates with lettuce and spoon on salad. Garnish with lemon and tomato wedges.

*S*erves 6.

# Lobster Salad Castine

*A* *piquant dressing gives zing to this simple but elegant salad. Serve with Herbed Pita Triangles.*

6 frozen lobster tails, cooked according to package directions, covered and chilled

3/4 cup extra-virgin olive oil

1/4 cup lime juice, or more to taste

Grated peel of 1 lime

1 teaspoon salt, or more to taste

1/2 teaspoon thyme

1/2 teaspoon ground cumin

1/2 cup minced green onions

1/4 cup minced parsley

1/2 teaspoon dried pepper flakes

6 hard-cooked eggs, quartered

4 tomatoes, thinly sliced

Whole Boston lettuce leaves, to line dinner plates

*I*n a small bowl, whisk oil, lime juice, grated lime peel, salt, thyme and cumin. Stir in onions, parsley and pepper flakes. Taste for seasoning and adjust.

*A*rrange lettuce leaves on six dinner plates, place lobster tails (with or without shells intact) in the center and garnish with quartered eggs and tomato slices. Drizzle dressing over all and pass remaining dressing in a small sauce boat.

*S*erves 6.

# Avocado Stuffed with Tuna and Chili Cream

*This is an adaptation of a most tasty salad that we enjoyed in a small cafe on the Baja coast.*

2 7-ounce cans water-packed tuna, drained, flaked and chilled

3 large, ripe avocados, halved, pitted and meat cut into small dice; reserve shells

Lemon juice, to brush inside reserved shells

1/2 cup coarsely chopped walnuts or pecans

1/2 cup heavy cream, whipped

1/2 cup bottled chili sauce

2 green onions, minced

Salt and pepper, to taste

Lettuce leaves, to line salad plates

1/2 cup finely chopped walnuts or pecans

Lemon wedges, for garnish

*In* a chilled bowl, whip cream until stiff, fold in chili sauce and onions. Refrigerate while preparing avocados.

*In* a medium bowl, combine chilled tuna, diced avocado, 1/2 cup nuts and cream/chili mixture. Add salt and pepper to taste. Pack generously into reserved avocado shells, set 1 shell on each lettuce-lined salad plate and garnish with chopped nuts and lemon wedges.

Serves 6.

# Low Calorie Tuna and Vegetable Salad

*You might like to precede this salad with a cup of cold cucumber-yogurt soup, which is also low in calories and fat.*

2 7-ounce cans water-packed tuna, drained and flaked

2 large sweet red peppers, cut into 2-inch julienne strips

2 medium carrots, scraped, cut into 2-inch x 1/4-inch strips

1 medium red onion, halved and sliced into thin crescents

1/2 cup small oil-cured olives

2/3 cup extra-virgin olive oil

3 tablespoons herb vinegar

2 tablespoons tomato paste

2 tablespoons minced fresh dillweed, or 1-1/2 teaspoons dried

1/2 teaspoon salt

1/2 teaspoon sugar

1/8 teaspoon hot pepper sauce, or more to taste

Shredded romaine lettuce, to line platter

Minced parsley, for garnish

Lemon wedges, for garnish

*B*lanch carrot sticks in boiling water for 1 minute, rinse with cold water and drain thoroughly.

*F*lake tuna into a large bowl, add peppers, carrots, onions and olives and toss together. Cover and chill while preparing dressing.

*I*n a small bowl, whisk together oil, vinegar, tomato paste, dill, salt, sugar and pepper sauce. Mix 1/2 cup dressing into tuna salad, taste for seasoning and adjust if necessary.

*L*ine a platter with shredded lettuce, mound salad on top, sprinkle with parsley and garnish with lemon wedges. Pass remaining dressing separately.

*S*erves 6.

# Garden Delight Tuna and Pasta Salad with Spinach Pesto

*A year-round favorite. Begin with carrot soup—hot or cold, depending on the season—and serve something chocolate for dessert.*

8 ounces rotelle pasta, cooked al dente, rinsed with cold water, drained and mixed with 1 tablespoon olive oil

13-ounce can tuna, drained and flaked in chunks

1-1/2 cups small broccoli florets

1 medium zucchini, scrubbed, halved lengthwise and thinly sliced

2 medium tomatoes, cut in thin wedges or 12 cherry tomatoes halved

1 small red onion, halved and thinly sliced

1/2 of 10-ounce box frozen spinach, thawed and water squeezed out

1/2 cup parsley leaves

1/4 cup pine nuts or walnuts

1/2 of 2-ounce tin anchovy fillets, drained and chopped

2 garlic cloves, chopped

1/2 teaspoon oregano, crushed

1/4 teaspoon salt, or more to taste

1/4 teaspoon freshly ground pepper, or more to taste

1/2 cup olive oil

Add to the bowl of food processor or blender jar spinach, parsley, nuts, anchovies, garlic, oregano, salt and pepper and whirl until smooth. While motor is running, slowly pour in oil and blend just until incorporated. Scrape into a small bowl and set aside, or refrigerate up to 1 week before using. Bring to room temperature before mixing with salad.

In a large bowl, combine pasta, tuna, broccoli, zucchini, tomatoes, onions and spinach pesto; toss until well mixed, cover and chill for 1 hour before serving.

Serves 6.

# Tuscany Tuna, Bean and Pasta Salad

*T*o the classic Italian bean and tuna salad we've added pasta. Serve with crunchy Italian bread or Focaccio bread, brushed with olive oil, sprinkled with minced garlic and parsley and warmed in the oven.

8 ounces small shell pasta, cooked al dente, rinsed with cold water and drained thoroughly

16-ounce can small white beans, drained and rinsed

7-ounce can oil-packed tuna, drained and broken into chunks

1 medium red onion, chopped

1/4 cup chopped parsley

2 tablespoons capers, drained

1/3 cup olive oil

3 tablespoons lemon juice

1 garlic clove, minced

1/2 teaspoon salt

1/4 teaspoon crushed red pepper flakes

1/2 teaspoon crushed sage leaves

*I*n a small bowl, whisk together oil, lemon juice, garlic, salt, pepper and sage. Taste for seasoning and adjust if necessary.

*A*dd pasta, beans, tuna, onion, parsley and capers to a large bowl, pour dressing over and mix well. Cover and refrigerate for several hours, stirring occasionally.

*S*erves 6.

# Tuna, Mushroom and Bacon Salad

*This has been a family favorite for years. Add a plate of sliced tomatoes sprinkled with fresh basil or dill and a basket of crunchy bread for a complete meal.*

4 cups torn iceberg and romaine lettuce
1/2 pound mushrooms, thinly sliced
1 cup thinly sliced green onions
13-ounce can oil-packed tuna, drained
6 slices bacon, crisply fried and crumbled
1 cup coarsely shredded Cheddar cheese
1/2 cup extra-virgin olive oil
1/4 cup lemon juice
2 garlic cloves, minced
1 teaspoon dry mustard
1/2 teaspoon salt
1/4 teaspoon freshly ground pepper

*I*n a small bowl, whisk together oil, lemon juice, garlic, mustard, salt and pepper; set aside.

*I*n a small bowl, mix bacon and cheese, cover and set aside.

*I*n a large salad bowl, layer the mixed greens, mushrooms and onions. Cover and refrigerate. These three steps can be done a few hours before serving time.

*J*ust before serving, break tuna into large chunks and add to the salad with reserved bacon/cheese mixture. Toss together, pour dressing over salad and toss again.

*S*erves 6.

# Pan Bagnat Nicoise

*This salad in bread is wonderful picnic fare, it's so self-contained.*

1 large, round, dense-type bread

2 garlic cloves, minced

Red wine vinegar and extra-virgin olive oil

1 small head iceberg lettuce, shredded

1 large ripe tomato, thinly sliced

7-ounce can oil-packed tuna, drained and flaked

1 small red onion, thinly sliced

2-ounce tin anchovy fillets, drained and chopped

30 Nicoise olives, pitted

6 radishes, thinly sliced

3 hard-cooked eggs, sliced

1 roasted large sweet red pepper, or small jar roasted peppers (Roast pepper under broiler until charred, place in a paper bag about 10 minutes; rub off skin and remove seeds. Slice into thin strips, add to small bowl with 1/4 cup olive oil and 6 fresh, torn basil leaves or 1/2 teaspoon dried basil, crushed. Marinate overnight.)

Salt and freshly ground pepper

3 tablespoons minced parsley

Slice top third of bread off, remove most of bread from bottom part of loaf, leaving a shell. Scatter garlic into bottom of bread and rub some into the top piece. Moisten bottom shell with vinegar and douse liberally with oil.

Layer lettuce, tomatoes, tuna, onion, anchovies, olives, radishes, eggs and roasted pepper in bottom of shell; pour oil/basil marinade over and sprinkle with salt, pepper and parsley. Put top of bread over salad and wrap tightly in plastic wrap. Set on a plate in the refrigerator and place a casserole or some other heavy object on top to weight down the bread/salad.

At serving time, remove the wrapping and slice into wedges.

Serves 6.

# Rice and Tuna Salad Provencal

*This flavorful salad should appeal to almost everyone, with its South of France seasonings and colors.*

2 cups cooked long-grain rice, chilled

16-ounce can white beans, rinsed and drained

13-ounce can oil-packed white tuna, drained

1/2 cup chopped sweet red or green pepper

1/2 cup chopped green onions

1/2 cup chopped fennel, if available (substitute chopped celery)

1/2 cup chopped, cured green olives

1/2 cup extra-virgin olive oil

1/4 cup tarragon vinegar

1 teaspoon salt

1/2 teaspoon thyme

1/2 teaspoon crushed fennel seeds (only if fresh fennel is unavailable)

1/4 teaspoon freshly ground pepper, or more to taste

Boston or bibb lettuce to line salad platter

3 hard-cooked eggs, quartered

3 medium tomatoes, sliced (vine-ripened only, otherwise eliminate)

*I*n a large bowl, gently mix together rice, beans, tuna, pepper, onions, fennel and olives.

*I*n a small bowl, whisk together oil, vinegar, salt, thyme, optional fennel seeds and pepper. Pour over salad, cover and chill for several hours.

*L*ine a platter or shallow bowl with lettuce, mix and taste salad for seasoning, adjust if necessary, and mound over lettuce. Garnish with eggs and tomatoes.

*S*erves 6.

# Chickpea, Tuna and Anchovy Salad

*This is quite literally an off-the-pantry-shelf salad; add Dann's Beer Bread or Beer Biscuits for a super simple meal.*

2 cups canned chickpeas, rinsed and drained

16-ounce can white beans, rinsed and drained

7-ounce can white tuna, drained and broken in chunks

2-ounce can anchovies, drained, soaked in milk, drained and chopped

1/2 cup extra-virgin olive oil

2 tablespoons lemon juice

1 tablespoon white wine vinegar

1 large garlic clove, minced

1/2 teaspoon rosemary, crushed

1/2 teaspoon salt, or more to taste

1/4 teaspoon freshly ground pepper, or more to taste

1 small red onion, thinly sliced and separated into rings, for garnish

3 tablespoons minced parsley, for garnish

*I*n a small bowl, whisk together oil, lemon juice, vinegar, garlic, rosemary, salt and pepper.

*I*n a large bowl, mix together chickpeas, beans, tuna, anchovies and dressing. Cover and chill several hours. Bring to room temperature and taste for seasoning before serving.

*L*ine an attractive bowl with lettuce leaves, spoon in salad and garnish with onion rings and parsley.

*S*erves 6.

# Middle East Eggplant, Tuna and Bulgur Wheat Salad

*E*ggplant, *long a Middle Eastern staple, has become a favorite of many American families, including ours. We hope it's one of yours, too.*

1 large eggplant, cut into 1-inch cubes

Salt

1/4 cup olive oil, or more as needed

1 each, large red and green sweet pepper, coarsely chopped

1 large onion, chopped

2 large garlic cloves, minced 3 tablespoons pine nuts, browned in oil

2 medium tomatoes, seeded and coarsely chopped

Salt and pepper to taste

1 cup plain yogurt

1 cup cooked bulgur wheat, chilled

7-ounce can oil-packed white tuna, drained and broken into chunks

1/4 cup minced parsley, for garnish

Lemon wedges, for garnish

*P*lace cubed eggplant in a colander, sprinkle generously with salt and let stand 30-40 minutes. Rinse with cold water and drain thoroughly, pat dry.

*H*eat olive oil in a large skillet, add peppers and onion and saute until almost soft; remove with a slotted spoon and set aside. Add more oil if necessary, heat and add eggplant. Toss occasionally until slightly browned, stir in garlic and cook 2 minutes more. Transfer to a large bowl, add pepper/onion mixture, pine nuts, tomatoes and salt and pepper to taste. Mix in bulgur wheat and tuna, cover and let stand at room temperature for at least 1 hour.

*B*efore serving, mix in yogurt, taste for seasoning and adjust if necessary.

*S*erves 6.

# Marinated Flounder, Potato and Pepper Salad

*A* *tasty potato salad made even tastier by the addition of marinated bits of flounder "cooked" in lemon juice, just as you prepare ceviche.*

1 pound flounder fillets, cut into 2 x 1-inch pieces (ask the fish counter person to remove the skin from the fillets)

1/2 cup lemon juice

1/4 cup extra-virgin olive oil

1 teaspoon salt

1/4 teaspoon crushed red pepper flakes

2 pounds red or wax-skin potatoes, scrubbed but not peeled

1/3 cup extra-virgin olive oil

3 tablespoons white wine vinegar

1 large garlic clove, minced

1/2 teaspoon rosemary, crushed

1/2 teaspoon salt

1/4 teaspoon freshly ground pepper

1/2 cup diced sweet green pepper

1/2 cup diced sweet red pepper

1/2 cup mayonnaise

1 tablespoon Dijon-style mustard

1/4 cup minced parsley

1/2 teaspoon salt

1/4 teaspoon freshly ground pepper

Minced parsley, for garnish

Snipped fresh rosemary, if available

*P*lace the flounder pieces in a shallow glass dish. In a small bowl, whisk together lemon juice, oil, salt and pepper flakes; pour over fish, cover and refrigerate about 4 hours.

*C*ook potatoes until soft and skins break. Drain and cool enough to handle, then slice thinly into a bowl containing the oil, vinegar, garlic, rosemary, salt and pepper; toss to coat. Cover and cool to room temperature.

*I*n a small bowl, mix together mayonnaise, mustard, parsley, salt and pepper.

*W*ith a slotted spoon, remove the fish from the marinade to the bowl with potatoes, add peppers and mayonnaise and gently toss to mix. Cover and chill for several hours. At serving time, transfer to an attractive bowl and sprinkle with parsley and snipped fresh rosemary, if available.

*S*erves 6.

# Flounder and Fresh Fruit Salad

*Delicate flounder combines with fresh fruit for an unusual appetizer or main course.*

2 pounds flounder fillets, poached 2 minutes in simmering water seasoned with 1 teaspoon salt, 6 peppercorns, 2 lemon wedges

1/2 pound seedless green grapes, halved if too large

1-1/2 cups small melon balls

2 large oranges, peeled and white pith removed, segments halved

1/4 cup mayonnaise

1/4 cup sour cream

3 tablespoons fresh lime juice

2 tablespoons honey

1 tablespoon minced fresh mint (do not use dried mint)

1-1/2 teaspoons grated ginger root (do not use powdered ginger)

Boston or bibb lettuce to line salad bowl

1/2 cup toasted sliced almonds, for garnish

Very thin slices of lime, for garnish

Clusters of fresh mint leaves, for garnish

*I*n a small bowl, stir together mayonnaise, sour cream, lime juice, honey, mint and ginger.

*C*hill poached fillets, then flake into a bowl containing grapes, melon balls and oranges. Pour dressing over salad and gently mix. Cover and refrigerate about 1 hour.

*T*o serve, line a bowl or platter with lettuce, spoon salad on top and garnish with almonds, lime slices and mint leaves.

*S*erves 6.

# Chilled Fried Fish with Ginger Vinaigrette

*C*risp *fried fish and vegetables, covered with a spicy soy vinaigrette, are an interesting alternative to a hot fried fish dinner.*

2 pounds cod or haddock fillets (or other thick whitefish)

1/3 cup flour, seasoned with 1/2 teaspoon salt, 1/4 teaspoon pepper, 1/4 teaspoon garlic powder

Olive oil for frying fish

3 medium carrots, scraped and cut into 2-inch lengths, then into thin strips

2 large red or green sweet peppers, cut into 2-inch lengths, then into thin strips

1/2 cup extra-virgin olive oil

1/4 cup soy sauce

2 tablespoons cider or red wine vinegar

2 tablespoons lemon juice

2 tablespoons minced onion

1 teaspoon grated fresh ginger root (do not use powdered)

1/4 teaspoon salt

1/4 teaspoon crushed red pepper flakes

Iceberg lettuce, sliced 1/2-inch wide, to line platter

Minced parsley, for garnish

Minced green onion tops, for garnish

*C*ut fish crosswise into 2-inch-wide pieces; toss in the seasoned flour. Heat oil in a large skillet over medium-high heat, add fish and fry a few at a time until both sides are lightly browned. Drain on paper toweling, place on a platter and chill about 30 minutes.

*I*n a small bowl, whisk together oil, soy sauce, vinegar, lemon juice, onion, ginger, salt and pepper flakes. Pour 1/2 cup vinaigrette over fish and return to refrigerator for at least 1 hour.

*P*lace carrot and pepper strips in separate bowls and pour remaining vinaigrette over them; cover and refrigerate.

*T*o serve salad, arrange lettuce strips on a large platter, remove fish from platter with a slotted spoon and arrange on lettuce. Remove carrots and peppers with a slotted spoon and arrange around fish. Pour marinade from vegetables over salad and garnish with parsley and green onions.

*S*erves 6.

# Provincetown Cod and Cucumber Salad

*This salad is so simple to prepare, it will leave you time to bake a batch of Peppery Cheese Biscuits—or buy some biscuits and spend some extra time at the beach.*

2 pounds cod fillets, poached, cooled and flaked

2 medium cucumbers, peeled and thinly sliced

1/2 cup mayonnaise

1/4 cup minced onion

2 tablespoons white wine vinegar

1 tablespoon horseradish

2 tablespoons minced fresh dill or 1-1/2 teaspoons dried

1/2 teaspoon sugar

1/2 teaspoon salt, or more to taste

1/4 teaspoon freshly ground pepper

3 hard-cooked eggs, quartered, for garnish

3 tablespoons minced green onion tops, for garnish

*P*lace cucumbers in a small bowl, sprinkle liberally with salt and let stand for 15 minutes. Rinse, drain and pat dry.

*I*n a salad bowl, toss together fish, cucumbers and dressing. Garnish with egg quarters and minced onions.

*S*erves 6.

# Boston Scrod and Potato Salad

*You don't have to be a Boston Brahmin to enjoy this salad.*

2 pounds new potatoes, scrubbed, cooked and diced

2 pounds scrod (or cod) fillets, poached in salted water, chilled and flaked in large pieces

1/2 cup extra-virgin olive oil

2 tablespoons vinegar

1 tablespoon white wine

1 tablespoon Dijon-style mustard

2 garlic cloves, minced

1/2 teaspoon salt, or more to taste

1/4 teaspoon freshly ground pepper, or more to taste

1/2 teaspoon thyme

1/4 cup minced parsley

1/4 cup minced green onions

2 tablespoons capers, drained

Romaine lettuce, to line salad bowl

*I*n a small bowl, whisk together oil, vinegar, wine, mustard, garlic, salt, pepper and thyme.

*A*dd diced warm potatoes to a large bowl, mix in 1/2 cup dressing and minced parsley. Cool to room temperature, stirring occasionally.

*A*dd remaining dressing, green onions and capers to flaked fish. Refrigerate at least 1 hour. Add fish to potatoes, taste for seasoning and adjust if necessary. Cover and chill for 1 hour.

*L*ine a large bowl with lettuce, add salad and serve.

Serves 6.

# Whitefish with Cucumbers and Lemon-Clam Sauce

*Here is an elegant salad to serve on that special occasion.*

2 pounds firm whitefish fillets (cod, haddock, snapper)

2 large cucumbers, peeled, halved lengthwise, seeded and cut into 1/4-inch slices

1 large carrot, coarsely shredded

3 tablespoons chopped fresh dill

2 tablespoons lemon juice

1/2 teaspoon salt

1/8 teaspoon freshly ground pepper

2 egg yolks

2 tablespoons lemon juice

2 teaspoons water

1 teaspoon corn starch

2/3 cup bottled clam juice

Salt and freshly ground pepper, to taste

Shredded iceberg lettuce, to line salad bowl

Minced dill, for garnish

Add fish to a large skillet, add cold water to half cover. Season water with 1 teaspoon salt, 6 peppercorns and 1 small bay leaf. Bring water to a simmer, remove from heat and keep fish in water until fish turns opaque. Remove to a platter, cover and chill.

When fish has cooled, flake into a large bowl, mix in cucumbers, carrots, dill, lemon juice, salt and pepper. Cover and chill for 1 hour.

In the top of a double boiler set over barely simmering water or in a small heavy saucepan, whisk together egg yolks, lemon juice and cornstarch mixed with water; cook just until mixture thickens. Scrape into a bowl and stir in clam juice. Chill and stir occasionally until cool and thick; add salt and pepper to taste.

To serve, line shallow bowl with shredded lettuce; mix salad with lemon-clam sauce and spoon on top of lettuce, then sprinkle with minced dill.

Serves 6.

# Whitefish and White Bean Salad

*A nutritious low-fat salad that provides plenty of protein and flavor.*

1-1/2 cups dried pea beans or navy beans, soaked overnight in 4 cups cold water

4 cups water, seasoned with 2 teaspoons salt, 1 bay leaf and 1 small onion stuck with 2 whole cloves

1/3 cup extra-virgin olive oil

1/4 cup tarragon vinegar

1 tablespoon minced fresh tarragon, or 1 teaspoon dried

1/2 teaspoon salt

1/4 teaspoon freshly ground pepper

1 medium red onion, chopped

1/2 cup chopped sweet red pepper

1/4 cup chopped oil-packed sun-dried tomatoes

2 pounds firm whitefish fillets (cod, haddock, snapper)

Water for poaching fish, mixed with 1/4 cup lemon juice and 1 teaspoon salt

2 tablespoons extra-virgin olive oil

2 tablespoons tarragon vinegar

Salt and freshly ground pepper, to taste

Minced parsley, for garnish

Minced tarragon, for garnish

*D*rain beans that have soaked overnight, rinse with cold water and add to saucepan with 4 cups seasoned water. Bring water to a boil, reduce heat and simmer beans, covered, 1 hour. Drain beans. In a large bowl, whisk together oil, vinegar, salt and pepper. Add beans, onion, pepper and sun-dried tomatoes, mix thoroughly and set aside to cool.

*P*lace fish in a large skillet, barely cover with water; add lemon juice and salt. Bring water to a simmer, poach fish 3 to 5 minutes. Remove to a platter, cover, and cool to room temperature.

*T*o serve, transfer beans to an attractive salad bowl, taste for seasoning and adjust if necessary. Flake fish into large chunks and place on top of beans; drizzle with oil and vinegar and sprinkle with salt and pepper. Garnish with parsley and tarragon.

*S*erves 6.

# Sea Trout, Green Bean and Potato Salad

*A Nicoise-type salad that uses economical sea trout.*

2 pounds sea trout fillets, poached in simmering water seasoned with 2 teaspoons salt, 6 peppercorns and 1/2 small onion

1 pound green beans, tipped and halved crosswise, simmered in salted water, 4-5 minutes, drained and patted dry

1 pound small, waxy potatoes, scrubbed and cooked in boiling salted water about 20 minutes or until soft, drained and sliced

1/2 cup extra-virgin olive oil

3 tablespoons white wine vinegar

2 garlic cloves, minced

1 teaspoon basil, crushed

1/2 teaspoon salt, or more to taste

1/4 teaspoon freshly ground pepper, or more to taste

1/2 cup chopped green onions

3 tablespoons chopped pimento

12 cured black olives

Red leaf lettuce to line platter or bowl

3 tomatoes, cut into wedges, for garnish

3 hard-cooked eggs, quartered, for garnish (optional)

*I*n a small bowl, whisk together oil, vinegar, garlic, basil, salt and pepper.

*R*emove the poached fish to a platter, cover and chill, then flake into large pieces; set aside.

*T*oss the warm beans with 3 tablespoons dressing, cover and cool to room temperature.

*T*oss warm sliced potatoes with 3 tablespoons dressing, cover and cool to room temperature.

*W*hen vegetables have cooled, combine in a large bowl fish, beans, potatoes, onions, pimento, olives and remaining dressing. Taste for seasoning and adjust if necessary. Cover and chill at least 1 hour.

*L*ine a salad bowl or platter with lettuce, mound salad in the center and surround with tomato wedges and eggs.

*S*erves 6.

# Pickled Bluefish or Sea Trout Salad

*You might serve as accompaniments to this salad a plate of your favorite deviled eggs and Parsley Skillet Bread.*

2-1/2 pounds bluefish or sea trout fillets, poached in salted water, cooled and flaked in large pieces

1/3 cup olive oil

3 carrots, scraped, cut into 2-inch lengths and thinly sliced

1 large sweet green pepper, thinly sliced

1 large sweet red pepper, thinly sliced

1 large onion, halved and thinly sliced

4 garlic cloves, minced

1/2 cup dry white wine

2 tablespoons vinegar

2 tablespoons raspberry vinegar (available at large supermarkets and specialty food stores)

1 teaspoon salt

1/2 teaspoon freshly ground pepper

1 bay leaf

1/2 teaspoon thyme

1/4 teaspoon coriander seeds, lightly crushed

Minced parsley, for garnish

*I*n a large skillet, heat oil over medium heat, add carrots, peppers and onions, and saute until vegetables are soft; do not brown. Just before removing from heat, add garlic and saute briefly. Transfer the vegetables to a bowl and stir in the wine, vinegar, raspberry vinegar, salt, pepper, bay leaf and thyme; cool to room temperature.

*L*ayer the cooled, flaked fish in a shallow glass dish with the cooled vegetables and marinade on top. Cover and chill overnight.

*T*o serve, taste the salad for seasoning and adjust if necessary, remove the bay leaf and spoon into an attractive bowl; sprinkle with parsley.

*S*erves 6.

# Poached Monkfish with Creamy Dressing

*E*uropeans refer to this fish as Lotte, but by either name it's a close substitute for lobster at half the price.

2-1/2 pounds monkfish, trimmed of membranes

Water to cover fish, flavored with 1 cup white wine, 1/4 cup vinegar, 2 teaspoons salt, 8 peppercorns, 1 bay leaf

2/3 cup mayonnaise

1/3 cup bottled chili sauce

2 tablespoons grated onion

1/2 teaspoon salt

1/8 teaspoon cayenne pepper

1/2 cup heavy cream, whipped

3 tablespoons minced parsley

Mixed iceberg and romaine lettuce, shredded, to line plates

Hard-cooked eggs, quartered, for garnish

Tomato wedges, for garnish

Nicoise or other black olives, for garnish

Watercress or parsley sprigs, for garnish

*P*lace monkfish in a large skillet; add seasoned water. Quickly bring to a boil, reduce heat so that water barely simmers and poach fish about 8 minutes or just until fish will flake with a fork. Cool the fish in the poaching liquor, remove to a platter and flake in large pieces. With a slotted spatula or spoon, transfer to a bowl, cover and chill 1 hour.

*I*n a medium bowl, mix together mayonnaise, chili sauce, onion, salt, cayenne, whipped cream and parsley. Adjust seasoning if necessary, cover and chill.

*T*o serve, line 6 dinner plates with mixed greens, divide the fish among them and spoon about 3 tablespoons dressing on top. Garnish each plate with eggs, tomatoes, olives and watercress sprigs. Pass remaining dressing separately.

*S*erves 6.

# Grilled Swordfish or Fresh Tuna Salad

*A* delicious way to enjoy grilled tuna or swordfish. Accompany with Herbed Pita Triangles.

1-1/2 pounds swordfish or tuna steaks

1 tablespoon extra-virgin olive oil and 2 teaspoons lemon juice to brush on fish

Salt and freshly ground pepper to season fish

16-ounce jar artichoke hearts, drained and quartered

16-ounce can hearts of palm, drained and sliced into 1/4-inch rounds

2/3 cup extra-virgin olive oil

1/4 cup red wine vinegar

1 tablespoon Dijon-style mustard

1 tablespoon fresh rosemary, chopped, or 1-1/2 teaspoons dried

2 garlic cloves, minced

1 teaspoon salt

1/4 teaspoon freshly ground pepper

6-ounce jar roasted red peppers, drained and thinly sliced

1/2 cup ripe olives

Romaine lettuce, torn into pieces, to line plates

1/2 bunch watercress, tough stems removed and roughly chopped

*I*n a small bowl, whisk together oil, vinegar, mustard, rosemary, garlic, salt and pepper.

*I*n a bowl, combine artichoke hearts and hearts of palm and 1/3 cup dressing. Marinate at least 1 hour. Before serving salad, add roasted peppers and olives to artichokes and hearts of palm; mix gently.

*A*bout 20 minutes before serving, brush fish with oil and lemon juice and sprinkle with salt and pepper. Place over hot coals or on a broiler pan, about 4 inches from the heat. Cook a total of 8 minutes on both sides. Remove to a platter, cool slightly and cut into 1-inch cubes.

*D*ivide fish cubes among 6 dinner plates that have been lined with romaine lettuce and watercress. Surround the fish with the vegetable mixture and drizzle with remaining dressing.

*S*erves 6.

# Salmon Steaks on Mixed Greens

*This is a very elegant salad but simple to prepare. Precede the salad with a cup of chilled soup and serve with one of our bread accompaniments.*

6 salmon steaks, cut 1/2-inch thick

1/4 cup unsalted butter

1 tablespoon salad oil

5-6 cups torn mixed salad greens: red leaf lettuce, arugula, Boston lettuce, radicchio, Belgian endive, spinach

1/2 cup extra-virgin olive oil

3 tablespoons walnut or hazelnut oil

1/4 cup sherry wine vinegar

1 tablespoon lemon juice

2 teaspoons Dijon-style mustard

1 garlic clove, minced

1 teaspoon salt

1/4 teaspoon freshly ground pepper

2 tablespoons minced green onions (white part only)

1 tablespoon toasted sesame seeds

Red caviar, for garnish

Lemon wedges, for garnish

*I*n a small bowl, whisk together olive oil, walnut oil, vinegar, lemon juice, mustard, garlic, salt and pepper. Stir in onions and sesame seeds.

*P*rior to preparing the salmon, toss the greens with the dressing. Line 6 dinner plates with salad greens.

*H*eat butter and oil (the oil will prevent the butter from browning too quickly at the high heat) in a large skillet. Add salmon steaks and sear quickly on both sides. The steaks should be almost opaque but still a bit pink near the bone. Place a steak in the center of each plate, spoon the butter from the skillet over each steak, garnish the salmon with caviar and place a wedge or two of lemon on the greens.

*S*erves 6.

# Salmon and Rice Salad

*This very tasty salad is a snap to prepare with canned salmon. Add a second salad of watercress, oranges and red onions for a meal full of flavor.*

4 cups warm cooked long-grain rice

3 cups flaked poached salmon, or 1 large and 1 small can red salmon, drained, skin and bones removed, and flaked

1 sweet red or green pepper, chopped

1 medium cucumber, peeled, seeded and chopped

1/2 cup chopped green onions

2 tablespoons minced fresh dillweed or 1-1/2 teaspoons dried

1/2 cup salad oil

1/4 cup mayonnaise

3 tablespoons lemon juice

2 teaspoons Dijon-style mustard, or more to taste

1 teaspoon salt

1/4 teaspoon freshly ground pepper

Minced parsley, grated lemon peel and fresh dill, mixed, for garnish

*In* a small bowl, mix together oil, mayonnaise, lemon juice, mustard, salt and pepper. Pour dressing over warm rice and mix thoroughly; cover and chill.

*In* a large salad bowl, toss together rice, salmon, pepper, cucumber, onions and dill. Cover and chill at least 1 hour. Taste for seasoning before serving. Garnish with parsley, lemon, and dill mixture.

*Serves 6.*

# Fresh Salmon and Pea Salad

*E*legant and colorful, this salad could be the centerpiece of a special summer dinner, especially if you can find fresh peas.

3 pounds salmon fillets

1 cup water

1 cup dry white wine

1 small onion, quartered

4 parsley sprigs

2 teaspoons salt

Cheesecloth bag containing: 1 bay leaf, 8 peppercorns, 1/2 teaspoon thyme, 1/2 teaspoon tarragon

1-1/2 cups cooked fresh peas, or 1-1/2 cup thawed frozen peas, blanched with boiling water, drained and chilled

1/2 cup thinly sliced radishes

1/2 cup extra-virgin olive oil

1/4 cup lemon juice

2 teaspoons Dijon-style mustard

2 tablespoons minced fresh dill or 1-1/2 teaspoons dried

1 garlic clove, minced

1 teaspoon salt

1/4 teaspoon freshly ground pepper

Boston or bibb lettuce, to line salad bowl

Fresh dill sprigs, for garnish

*I*n a large skillet, combine water, wine, onion, parsley, salt and garni-bag. Bring to a boil, reduce heat and simmer 10 minutes. Add salmon and water to almost cover and barely simmer for 8 minutes or until fish just begins to flake when tested with a fork. Remove with a slotted spatula to a platter, remove skin and any bones and flake into 1-inch pieces. Transfer to a bowl, cover and chill at least 1 hour.

*I*n a large bowl, whisk together oil, lemon juice, mustard, dill, garlic, salt and pepper. Add chilled salmon, peas and radishes and mix gently.

*L*ine a salad bowl with lettuce and spoon the salad in the center; garnish with dill sprigs.

*S*erves 6.

# Poached Salmon Steaks with Cucumber Dressing

*S*almon and cucumber have a special affinity. As a buffet dish, the salmon could be flaked into larger pieces and tossed with the dressing.

6 salmon steaks, 1/2-inch thick, poached in simmering water seasoned with salt, 6 peppercorns, 1 bay leaf, 1/2 lemon

3 medium cucumbers, peeled, seeded and coarsely shredded

1 cup mayonnaise

1/2 cup sour cream

1 tablespoon lemon juice

1 tablespoon minced fresh dill, or 1 teaspoon dried

1 tablespoon minced parsley

1 tablespoon grated onion

1/2 teaspoon salt, or more to taste

1/4 teaspoon freshly ground pepper

Iceberg lettuce, sliced 1/2-inch wide, to line plates

Cherry tomatoes, for garnish

Very thin carrot sticks, for garnish

Chopped parsley, for garnish

*T*ransfer poached salmon, with a slotted spatula, to a platter; remove skin and center bone, leaving steak intact. Cover and chill at least 1 hour.

*I*n a small bowl, combine shredded cucumbers, mayonnaise, sour cream, lemon juice, dill, parsley, onion, salt and pepper. Cover and chill 1 hour. Taste for seasoning before serving.

*L*ine 6 salad plates with lettuce, place a salmon steak in the center and spoon dressing lavishly onto each steak. Garnish with cherry tomatoes (sliced in half if large), carrots and parsley. Pass remaining dressing separately.

*S*erves 6.

# Salt Codfish and Potato Salad

*Another fish and potato salad, this one with salt codfish. If you've never had salt codfish before, you'll be delighted with the flavor.*

2 pounds salt codfish, soaked overnight in cold water

3 pounds red or wax-skinned potatoes, scrubbed and boiled in salted water until just tender, cooled and sliced

2 medium red onions, thinly sliced

1/2 cup chopped parsley

3/4 cup extra-virgin olive oil

1/4 cup vinegar

1 teaspoon thyme

1/2 teaspoon freshly ground pepper

Salt to taste

1 tablespoon capers, drained, for garnish

Minced parsley, for garnish

*D*rain codfish, put into a skillet with water to cover and poach just until fish flakes when tested with a fork. Remove with a slotted spatula to a platter, cool and flake in chunks.

*I*n a small bowl, whisk together oil, vinegar, thyme and pepper.

*I*n a shallow bowl, layer half the codfish, potatoes and onions with a sprinkling of parsley between each layer. Pour half the dressing over the salad. Layer remaining fish, potatoes and onions, with parsley sprinkled between each layer; pour remaining dressing on top, cover and let stand about 30 minutes at room temperature before serving. Salad can be prepared ahead of time and refrigerated, but should be brought to room temperature before serving. Taste for salt and garnish with capers and parsley.

*S*erves 6.

# Black Sea Herring, Ham and Egg Salad

*Serve this salad with thick slices of pumpernickel bread slathered with sweet butter, and mugs of cold beer.*

3 pickled herring fillets, diced in 1/2-inch pieces, or 2 cups jarred pickled herring, drained and diced

1/2 pound thickly sliced baked ham, diced

4 hard-cooked eggs, chopped

2 medium potatoes, cooked, peeled and diced

1 large red apple, cored and diced

1 large dill pickle, diced

1 cup sour cream

2 tablespoons white wine vinegar

1 tablespoon prepared mustard

1 tablespoon horseradish

1 teaspoon sugar, or more to taste

1 teaspoon dillweed

1/2 teaspoon salt, or more to taste

Iceberg lettuce, torn into pieces, to line platter or bowl

*In* a small bowl, mix together sour cream, vinegar, mustard, horseradish, sugar and salt. Taste for seasoning and adjust if necessary.

*In* a large bowl, mix together herring, ham, eggs, potatoes, apple, pickle and dressing. Cover and chill at least 1 hour.

*Line* a platter or shallow bowl with lettuce, mound salad on top and sprinkle with paprika.

*Serves 6.*

# Pickled Herring, Potato and Beet Salad

*In this era of* glasnost, *this Russian-style salad should appeal to many.*

16-ounce jar pickled herring, drained and cut into 1-inch pieces

4 medium potatoes, cooked, peeled and sliced

16-ounce jar pickled beets, drained and diced

1 medium red onion, thinly sliced

1/3 cup red wine vinegar

2 tablespoons olive oil

3 tablespoons sugar, or more to taste

1/2 teaspoon thyme

Salt and freshly ground pepper to taste

Romaine lettuce leaves, to line platter

6 hard-cooked eggs, halved

Sweet paprika

Minced fresh dill or parsley, for garnish

*In* a large bowl, mix together herring, potatoes, beets and onion.

*In* a small bowl, dissolve sugar in vinegar, add oil and thyme. Mix into salad and taste for salt and pepper, adjust if necessary. Cover and let marinate at room temperature up to 1 hour, then refrigerate for several hours. Salad can be prepared up to 3 days before serving.

*To* serve, line a platter with lettuce leaves, mound salad in the center and arrange eggs around salad. Sprinkle with paprika and garnish with minced fresh dill or parsley.

*S*erves 6.

# Poultry Salads

# Poultry Salads

*Leftover chicken or turkey—or poultry cutlets straight from the grill— play starring roles in some of the tastiest, heartiest salads around. A tip if your recipe calls for poached chicken: never let the poaching liquid come to a boil—a slight surface shimmer results in succulent, tender chicken every time.*

# Chicken and Potato Salad with Basil Mayonnaise

*A*nchovy Toasts *would add another piquant flavor to this meal.*

3 chicken breast halves, cooked, skinned and meat shredded, or 3 cups of leftover chicken

2 cups diced, cooked potatoes

1 cup thinly sliced celery

1/2 cup chopped green onion tops

1/2 cup packed fresh basil leaves

1/4 cup parsley, stems removed

1/2 teaspoon salt

1/4 teaspoon freshly ground pepper

2 tablespoons olive oil

2 tablespoons basil or white wine vinegar

1 large garlic clove, quartered

1/2 teaspoon salt

1/4 teaspoon freshly ground pepper

1/2 cup mayonnaise

3 garden-fresh tomatoes, thinly sliced, or 18 small cherry tomatoes, for garnish

Basil leaves, for garnish

*C*ombine chicken, potatoes, celery and onions in a large bowl; sprinkle with 1/2 teaspoon salt and 1/4 teaspoon freshly ground pepper.

*A*dd to food processor bowl or blender basil leaves, parsley, garlic, salt and pepper and blend until smooth. Blend in the oil and vinegar. Scrape into a small bowl and stir in the mayonnaise. Pour over the salad ingredients and mix thoroughly. Cover and refrigerate at least 2 hours.

*A*t serving time, taste for seasoning and adjust, transfer to a shallow bowl and arrange the tomato slices and basil leaves around the edge of the salad.

*S*erves 6.

# Block Party Rice and Chicken Salad

*This recipe can easily be doubled, can be prepared the day before serving and looks terrific on a picnic table.*

1 cup raw rice, cooked to package directions

4 chicken breast halves, poached, cooled and shredded

1 small sweet red pepper, julienned

1 small sweet green pepper, julienned

1 small red onion, finely chopped

4 green onions, tops only, minced

1 small jar marinated artichoke hearts, drained and quartered

1 cup frozen tiny peas, thawed and blanched with boiling water

1/2 cup pitted black olives, halved

1/4 cup chopped parsley

2 tablespoons minced fresh dillweed or 1 teaspoon dried dill

Salt and pepper to taste

1 cup olive oil

1/3 cup red wine vinegar

2 tablespoons Dijon-style mustard

1 tablespoon minced parsley

1 garlic clove, minced

1 teaspoon sugar

1 teaspoon salt

1/2 teaspoon freshly ground pepper

*W*hile rice is cooking, whisk together in a small bowl the oil, vinegar, mustard, parsley, garlic, sugar, salt and pepper. Transfer hot rice to a large bowl, pour 3/4 cup dressing over the rice and mix gently. Set aside and cool to room temperature. Reserve remaining dressing.

*W*hen rice is cool, add shredded chicken, peppers, red onion, onion tops, artichokes, peas, olives, parsley, dill, some of the reserved dressing if necessary, and salt and pepper to taste. Mix thoroughly, cover with plastic wrap and refrigerate several hours or overnight.

*A*t serving time, add the reserved dressing as needed and taste for seasoning. Transfer to an attractive serving bowl.

*S*erves 6.

# Sweet and Tangy Chicken Salad

*S*auteed chicken breasts, sliced on the diagonal, give a special look and taste to this fruited chicken salad.

4 boneless and skinless chicken breast halves

Salt and lemon pepper for seasoning

1/2 cup seedless green grapes, halved

1 cup chicken broth, all fat removed

3/4 cup dry white wine, divided

1 tablespoon lemon juice

1/2 teaspoon salt

1/4 teaspoon lemon pepper

2 teaspoons Dijon-style mustard

1 garlic clove, minced

1/3 cup extra-virgin olive oil

1/4 cup walnut oil (available in large supermarkets and specialty food stores)

1/2 pound fresh spinach leaves, well rinsed, tough stems removed and spun or patted dry

1 cup shredded iceberg lettuce (use crisp center leaves)

1/2 cup seedless green grapes, halved, for garnish

1/2 cup coarsely chopped toasted walnuts, for garnish

*A*dd grapes, chicken broth, 1/2 cup wine, lemon juice, salt and pepper to food processor bowl or blender and blend until smooth. Transfer to a small saucepan and bring to a boil, reduce heat and simmer for 5 minutes. Transfer to a small bowl and whisk in remaining 1/4 cup wine, mustard, garlic and olive and walnut oils. Set aside while preparing chicken.

*H*eat a large skillet over high heat, add just enough salad oil to film the bottom, then add chicken breasts and quickly sear one side. Use a spatula and fork to turn, sprinkle with salt and lemon pepper and sear second side. Remove to a platter and slice into 1/2-inch diagonal strips. Transfer to a bowl and pour the reserved marinade over the chicken. Marinate at least 1 hour, at room temperature, before serving.

*A*t serving time, place the spinach leaves and lettuce in a large bowl or platter. With a slotted spoon, transfer the chicken to the bowl or platter. Pour any marinade over the platter, scatter the grapes on top and sprinkle with walnuts.

*S*erves 6.

# Canton Chicken Salad

*A hot Oriental chicken salad is sure to perk up sagging winter appetites.*

1 large head iceberg lettuce, shredded

1 cup thinly sliced celery

1/4 cup chopped parsley

1 small can chow mein noodles

1/4 cup salad oil

4 boneless and skinless chicken breast halves, cut into 2 x 1/2- inch strips

1/4 pound fresh snow peas, tipped, strings removed and cut in half

7-ounce can water chestnuts, drained and sliced

2 tablespoons rice wine or dry white wine

2 tablespoons lemon juice

2 tablespoons brown sugar

1 tablespoon curry powder, or to taste

1 tablespoon soy sauce

1 garlic clove, minced

1/2 teaspoon minced fresh ginger root

1-1/2 cups mayonnaise

8 radishes, thinly sliced, for garnish

4 green onions, minced, for garnish

1/4 cup chopped cashew nuts or peanuts

*I*n a large salad bowl, toss together lettuce, celery and parsley; sprinkle chow mein noodles on top and set aside.

*I*n a small bowl, mix together the wine, lemon juice, sugar, curry powder, soy sauce, garlic and ginger root. Add the mayonnaise and stir until smooth; set aside while preparing chicken.

*H*eat oil in a wok or large skillet until very hot, add chicken and stir-fry until golden. Add snow peas and water chestnuts and stir-fry another minute or until heated through. Remove with a slotted spoon to the lettuce bowl. Add 1 cup of dressing and toss to coat. Garnish with the radishes, onions and nuts. Serve immediately and pass the remaining dressing separately.

*S*erves 6.

# Chicken Waldorf Salad

*This salad is a variation of a childhood favorite. Serve with the bread or rolls of your choice, but the Easy Cheddar Braid has been a nice accompaniment.*

4 chicken breast halves

3 cups chicken broth or water seasoned with a small onion, 1 stalk celery, 6 peppercorns, 2 teaspoons salt and 1 bay leaf

3 medium red apples, cored and diced (do not peel)

1 cup thinly sliced celery

1/2 cup raisins, plumped in 2 tablespoons each dry sherry and hot water

1/2 cup finely chopped parsley

1/2 cup mayonnaise

1/2 cup sour cream

1 tablespoon lemon juice

1/4 teaspoon salt

1/4 teaspoon ground cinnamon

1 head Boston lettuce, separated into whole leaves

1/4 cup olive oil and lemon juice, mixed, to sprinkle on lettuce

1/2 cup chopped, toasted walnuts, for garnish

2 tablespoons minced parsley, for garnish

*A*dd broth or seasoned water to a large skillet and bring to a boil. Add chicken breasts, reduce heat and simmer about 15 minutes. Remove to a platter, cover with plastic wrap and cool to room temperature. Reserve broth for another use.

*M*ix mayonnaise, sour cream, lemon juice, salt and cinnamon together in a small bowl; set aside while preparing salad.

*W*hen chicken is cool, remove skin and bones and cut into small pieces. Add to a large bowl with the apples, celery, raisins and parsley. Add reserved dressing and mix thoroughly. Taste for salt and adjust. Cover and refrigerate for at least 2 hours before serving.

*A*t serving time, line 6 dinner plates with lettuce leaves, sprinkle with the vinaigrette and divide the chicken salad among the plates. Garnish with walnuts and parsley.

*S*erves 6.

# Monterey Chicken Salad

*We enjoyed a similar salad last year in California. Chilled cream of broccoli soup makes a great first course.*

1 3-pound chicken (or breasts and thighs only), cooked, skinned and boned and shredded into small pieces

1 cup thinly sliced celery

1/2 cup coarsely grated carrots

1 small jar marinated artichoke hearts, drained and halved

1 ripe avocado, peeled, pitted and diced and tossed with 2 teaspoons lemon juice

3/4 cup extra-virgin olive oil

3 tablespoons white wine vinegar

1 tablespoon prepared mustard

1/2 teaspoon salt, or more to taste

1 tablespoon chopped fresh tarragon or 1 teaspoon dried, crushed

Romaine lettuce, thinly sliced, for garnish

*I*n a large bowl, whisk together olive oil, vinegar, mustard, salt and tarragon. Add shredded chicken and marinate 1 hour at room temperature.

*A*t serving time, scatter lettuce on a round platter. Remove chicken from the marinade with a slotted spoon and mound in the center of the platter. Add the prepared vegetables to the marinade and toss to coat. Remove with a slotted spoon and arrange around the chicken on the platter. Pour the remaining marinade into a small bowl and serve separately.

*S*erves 6.

# Hunan Chicken Salad

*Your family or guests will enjoy the double taste-treat of sampling this salad with two different dressings.*

3 cups chicken broth

2 pounds boneless chicken breasts

1 medium onion, thinly sliced

1 star anise (available in Oriental food stores)

1/4-inch-wide slice fresh ginger root

1 tablespoon soy sauce

1 tablespoon salad oil

1 teaspoon white wine vinegar

1/4 pound fresh bean sprouts, rinsed and drained

1/4 pound snow peas, strings removed and sliced lengthwise

1 large sweet red pepper, thinly sliced lengthwise

1 large carrot, cut into 2-inch pieces, then julienned

*Spicy Honey Sesame Dressing*

6 tablespoons Chinese sesame paste (do not use tahini)

4 tablespoons soy sauce

2 teaspoons hoisin sauce (available in Oriental food stores)

2 teaspoons hot chili oil (available in Oriental food stores and large supermarkets)

3 tablespoons honey

2 tablespoons sesame oil

Warm water, as needed

*Mustard Sesame Dressing*

1/4 cup Dijon-style mustard

1/4 cup sesame oil

1/4 cup salad oil

2 tablespoons white wine vinegar

1 tablespoon dry sherry

Salt to taste

*A*dd chicken broth, onion, star anise and ginger to a large saucepan and bring to a boil. Reduce heat, add chicken breasts, and simmer, uncovered, 15 minutes. Remove from the heat and cool chicken in the broth.

*B*lanch bean sprouts in boiling water about 15 seconds, rinse with cold water, drain thoroughly and set aside. Blanch prepared snowpeas in boiling water about 20 seconds, rinse with cold water, drain thoroughly and set aside. Prepare red pepper and carrot and set aside.

*P*repare dressings separately by whisking together all ingredients for each. To the Spicy Honey Sesame Dressing, add enough warm water to make a thick but pourable dressing. Dressings can be prepared up to 1 week ahead, but bring to room temperature and taste for seasoning before serving.

After chicken has cooled, remove from the broth and remove skin. Shred chicken into thin strips. Mix together the soy sauce, salad oil and vinegar and pour over the chicken. Toss to coat. Mound the chicken in the center of a large platter and sprinkle with sesame seeds. Arrange the vegetables around the chicken in separate mounds. Pass the dressings in small bowls.

Serves 6.

# Chicken and Broccoli with Tarragon Dressing

*This salad is essentially made up of two main ingredients, so your shopping list will be short. You might like to add a basket of crisp Anchovy Toasts to serve with the salad.*

4 boneless chicken breasts, simmered 15 minutes in water seasoned with 1 small onion, 1 stalk celery, 1 small carrot, 1 bay leaf, 2 teaspoons salt and 6 peppercorns

4 cups broccoli florets

1 cup diced broccoli stems

Boiling salted water

1 cup mayonnaise

1/2 cup sour cream

1 tablespoon white wine vinegar

1 tablespoon chopped fresh tarragon or 1 teaspoon dried

1/2 teaspoon salt

1/4 teaspoon freshly ground pepper

Chopped parsley, for garnish

Chopped fresh tarragon, if available, for garnish

After the chicken breasts are cooked, remove them to a plate, cover with plastic wrap and cool slightly. Discard the skin; cut meat into 1-inch cubes. Place in a bowl and set aside.

Cook the broccoli in the boiling water for 3 minutes, drain in a colander, then place on paper toweling and pat dry. Add to the chicken.

In a small bowl, mix together the mayonnaise, sour cream, vinegar, tarragon and salt and pepper. Pour 1 cup dressing over the chicken and broccoli and mix thoroughly. Cover salad and chill for several hours. Add additional dressing, if necessary, before serving.

Transfer to an attractive salad bowl and taste for seasoning, then sprinkle with parsley and tarragon before serving.

Serves 6.

# Roast Chicken and Potato Salad a la Reine

*The next time you're planning to serve roast chicken, do up an extra one and make this salad a day or two later.*

3 pounds chicken, roasted with 1 lemon, parsley sprigs, 1 teaspoon rosemary, salt and pepper
Melted butter or olive oil to brush on chicken
2 pounds red or wax skin potatoes
1/4 cup white wine vinegar
1/4 cup white wine
1/2 teaspoon rosemary, crushed
1 cup frozen tiny peas, thawed and blanched with boiling water

5 green onions, thinly sliced
1 cup mayonnaise
2 tablespoons fresh lemon juice
3 tablespoons minced parsley
Salt and pepper to taste
3 tomatoes, quartered, for garnish
1 sweet green pepper, sliced into rings, for garnish

*R*inse chicken inside and out and sprinkle cavity with salt and pepper. Place lemon, halved, parsley sprigs and rosemary inside cavity. Put chicken on a large square of foil, brush with butter or oil and bring up ends of foil to enclose chicken. Set the package in a shallow pan and roast in a 400-degree oven for 1 hour and 15 minutes. Remove the chicken to a platter and reserve juices. Cool chicken, then cover and refrigerate.

*P*eel and slice potatoes 1/2-inch thick, then cut into 1/4-inch sticks. Cook in boiling, salted water for barely 5 minutes. Drain and transfer to a large bowl, toss immediately with the vinegar, wine and rosemary; set aside to cool, then cover and refrigerate.

*R*emove any fat from reserved juices, pour into a small saucepan and heat, then strain through a lined sieve. Mix 1/2 cup of the juice into the mayonnaise, lemon juice and parsley and add salt and pepper to taste.

*R*emove the chicken from the refrigerator and discard skin. Remove all meat from the bones and cut into bite-size pieces. To the cooled potatoes, add chicken, peas, onions and dressing; mix gently but thoroughly. Taste for salt and pepper and adjust. Transfer to a shallow bowl or platter and garnish with tomato wedges and pepper rings.

*S*erves 6.

# Mandarin Chicken and Noodle Salad

*Precede this salad with small bowls of clear chicken broth garnished with shreds of green onion tops and shredded carrots. Use the broth from the cooked chicken breasts.*

4 chicken breast halves, cooked, skinned, boned and shredded

2 cups shredded Chinese cabbage

6 green onions, thinly sliced

1/2 sweet red pepper, thinly sliced

3 ounces Chinese rice noodles

1/4 cup salad oil

3 tablespoons white wine vinegar

2 tablespoons soy sauce

1 tablespoon sesame oil

1 tablespoon sugar

1 teaspoon dry mustard

1 teaspoon grated ginger root

1 garlic clove, minced

Salt and pepper to taste

1/4 cup minced parsley, for garnish

1 tablespoon toasted sesame seeds, for garnish

*I*n a large bowl, combine the chicken, cabbage, onions and red pepper. Cover and chill while cooking noodles and preparing dressing.

*C*ook noodles according to package directions, drain and rinse with cold water and drain thoroughly, set aside.

*W*hisk dressing ingredients together in a small bowl. Pour over chilled chicken and vegetables and mix thoroughly. Add noodles and mix again. Transfer to a serving bowl and garnish with parsley and sesame seeds.

*S*erves 6.

# Curried Chicken-Pecan Salad

*Serve this salad open-face on toasted croissant halves or slices of Easy Cheddar Braid.*

4 boneless chicken breast halves, poached in seasoned simmering water for 15 minutes

1/2 cup coarsely chopped toasted pecans

1/2 cup thinly sliced celery

2 tablespoons grated onion

1/2 cup mayonnaise

3 tablespoons sour cream

2 tablespoons chopped chutney

1 teaspoon curry powder, or more to taste

Salt to taste

Chutney to spread on croissants or bread of your choice

Cucumber sticks, for garnish

*C*ool chicken breasts, then cut into small cubes. Reserve broth and use for soup to serve with salad, if desired. Mix chicken, pecans, celery and onion together.

*I*n a small bowl, mix mayonnaise, sour cream, chutney, curry powder and salt to taste. Mix into salad ingredients, cover and chill for several hours or overnight.

*A*t serving time, spread chutney and salad on croissants or bread and place on salad plates. Garnish with cucumber sticks.

*S*erves 6.

# Dilly Chicken and Potato Salad

*C*ontinue the dill theme by serving a side dish of cherry tomatoes,
rolled in olive oil, dillweed and salt and pepper, then baked in a 400-
degree oven just until the tomato skin starts to split.

4 chicken breast halves, poached in
seasoned water, skinned, boned and cut in
bite-size pieces

4 red or wax potatoes, boiled, peeled and
sliced

1/2 cup chopped dill pickles

1/2 cup celery, thinly sliced

4 green onions, thinly sliced

2 tablespoons capers, drained

1/2 cup mayonnaise

1/2 cup sour cream

2 tablespoons pickle juice

1/2 teaspoon dillweed

1/2 teaspoon salt, or more to taste

1/4 teaspoon freshly-ground pepper, or more
to taste

Boston or bibb lettuce to line platter

3 hard-cooked eggs, quartered, for garnish

12 pitted green olives, quartered, for
garnish

*I*n a large bowl, mix together chicken, potatoes, pickles, celery,
onions and capers. Cover and set aside.

*I*n a small bowl, mix mayonnaise, sour cream, pickle juice, dillweed,
salt and pepper. Taste for seasoning and adjust. Add to salad
ingredients and mix thoroughly. Cover and chill.

*A*t serving time, transfer to a platter lined with lettuce leaves and
garnish with quartered eggs; scatter olives on top of salad.

*S*erves 6.

# Janice's Layered Chicken Salad

*This is definitely a "make the day before" salad.*

3 boneless, skinless chicken breast halves,
poached in salted water, cooled and
shredded

1 small head iceberg lettuce, torn into pieces

1 medium red onion, halved and thinly sliced

1/2 cup thinly sliced celery

1/2 cup chopped sweet green pepper

1/4 cup chopped parsley

1 cup frozen peas, thawed

1-1/2 cups mayonnaise

2 tablespoons sugar

2 cups shredded Cheddar cheese

8 slices bacon, crisply fried and crumbled,
for garnish

Salt and pepper to taste

*P*lace the lettuce in a large ceramic bowl, then layer in the following order: onion, celery, chicken, green pepper, parsley and peas. Spread with mayonnaise and sprinkle with sugar. Scatter cheese on top, then cover tightly with plastic wrap and refrigerate overnight.

*A*t serving time, sprinkle salad with salt and pepper and scatter bacon on top; toss at the table.

*S*erves 6.

# Puff Bowl with Chicken and Cucumber Salad

*Your family or guests will be amused by this salad in its own bowl.*

Puff Bowl (see page 21)

4 chicken breast halves, poached in seasoned water, cooled, skin and bones removed, and meat cut into small pieces

1 medium cucumber, peeled and diced

1/4 cup thinly sliced celery

1/4 cup julienne slices sweet red or green pepper

2 tablespoons minced parsley

1 cup extra-virgin olive oil

1/4 cup herbed vinegar

1 tablespoon Dijon-style mustard

1 teaspoon tarragon, crushed

1 teaspoon salt

1/4 teaspoon freshly ground pepper

1 quarter head iceberg lettuce, shredded

Thin slices red onion, for garnish

Whole small or halved ripe olives, for garnish

Capers, for garnish

*P*repare Puff Bowl in advance.

*C*ombine chicken, cucumber, celery, peppers and parsley.

*I*n a small bowl, whisk together oil, vinegar, mustard, tarragon, salt and pepper. Pour 2/3 cup dressing over salad ingredients and toss to mix. Cover and refrigerate until lightly chilled.

*A*t serving time, line Puff Bowl with lettuce. Taste salad for seasoning and adjust, then transfer to Puff Bowl. Arrange onions and olives attractively on salad and scatter with capers. Pass remaining dressing.

*S*erves 6.

# Paella Chicken Salad

*Here is a chilled version of a favorite Spanish entree. Serve with crusty Italian bread and a pitcher of red or white sangria.*

1 cup long grain rice, sauteed in oil and cooked following package directions

2 cups shredded cooked chicken

1/2 pound medium shrimp, simmered for 3 minutes in 1-1/2 cups water seasoned with 1 teaspoon salt and 2 teaspoons pickling spice

2 hot Italian sausages, cooked and thinly sliced

1 large tomato, seeded and chopped

1/2 cup frozen tiny peas, thawed and blanched with boiling water

1/2 cup thinly sliced celery

1/4 cup minced onion

12 small pimento olives

3 tablespoons minced cilantro or parsley

1/2 cup olive oil

3 tablespoons red wine vinegar

1/2 teaspoon curry powder

1/2 teaspoon dry mustard

1/2 teaspoon salt, or more to taste

1/4 teaspoon freshly ground pepper

Romaine lettuce, for lining bowl

Tomato slices, for garnish

Lime wedges, for garnish

*I*n a small bowl, whisk together the oil, vinegar, curry powder, dry mustard, salt and pepper.

*T*ransfer cooked rice to a large bowl and pour 1/2 cup dressing over rice. Set aside to cool to room temperature.

*A*fter cooked shrimp cool, peel and add to cooled rice. Add chicken, sausage, tomato, peas, celery, onion, olives and cilantro to bowl and toss to mix. Add remaining dressing and taste for seasoning; adjust to taste.

*L*ine a platter or shallow bowl with lettuce, top with salad and garnish with tomato slices and lime wedges. Serve at room temperature or lightly chilled.

*S*erves 6.

# Greek-Isle Chicken and Rice Salad

*Chicken and rice are traditional at Greek wedding feasts. Weddings aside, this salad is a feast in itself.*

3 cups cooked long-grain rice, chilled

3 cups bite-size cooked chicken

1/2 of 10-ounce bag fresh spinach, rinsed, patted dry and thinly sliced

6 green onions, thinly sliced

1 cup plain yogurt

1/2 cup mayonnaise

1 tablespoon lemon juice

1 tablespoon olive oil

1 garlic clove, minced

1 teaspoon oregano, crushed

1 teaspoon salt

1/4 teaspoon freshly ground pepper, or more to taste

Mixed greens, to line salad bowl

Cured black olives, for garnish

Chopped fresh mint, for garnish (do not use dried mint)

Combine in a large bowl the rice, chicken, spinach and onions.

In a small bowl, mix together yogurt, mayonnaise, lemon juice, oil, garlic, oregano, salt and pepper. Pour 1 cup over salad and mix thoroughly. Cover and chill at least 2 hours before serving. Add more dressing if necessary.

Line an attractive bowl with lettuce; taste salad for seasoning and adjust if necessary, mound on top of lettuce and garnish with olives and mint.

Serves 6.

# Chicken and White Bean Salad with Tahini Dressing

*A* *salad with Middle Eastern overtones. If you're especially fond of chickpeas, use them in place of the white beans.*

4 chicken breast halves, cooked, skin and bones removed, and meat pulled into small pieces

3 cups canned white beans

1 cup diced sweet red or green pepper

1/2 cup thinly sliced green onions

1/3 cup chopped parsley

1/2 cup crumbled feta cheese

1/2 cup tahini (available in Middle Eastern food stores or large supermarkets)

1/2 cup fresh lemon juice

2 tablespoons water

1 teaspoon basil or oregano, crushed

1 teaspoon salt

1/4 teaspoon freshly ground pepper

Shredded escarole or romaine for lining bowl

Cured black olives for garnish

Chopped fresh basil or oregano, for garnish if available (do not use dried)

*C*ombine in a large bowl chicken, beans, diced pepper, onions, parsley and feta cheese. Cover and chill while preparing dressing.

*I*n a small bowl, mix together tahini, lemon juice, water, basil or oregano, salt and pepper. Pour over salad, toss and taste for seasonings; adjust if necessary. Serve salad at room temperature or lightly chilled. Before serving, line a bowl with lettuce, mound salad on top and garnish with olives and fresh herbs, if available.

*S*erves 6.

# Grilled Chicken and Salad Greens

*This salad is both a feast for your palate and your eyes. The hot chicken breasts contrast deliciously with crisp greens.*

6 small boneless and skinless chicken breast halves, pounded to 1/2-inch thickness

1/4 cup olive oil

1/4 cup lemon juice

1 teaspoon dried rosemary, crushed

4 medium tomatoes, seeded and diced

1 small onion, chopped

2 garlic cloves, minced

1 cup olive oil

2 tablespoons lemon juice

1 teaspoon salt, or more to taste

1/2 teaspoon freshly ground pepper

1 teaspoon sugar

1 head romaine lettuce, rinsed and tough spine removed, cut into 1/2-inch slices

1 bunch watercress, rinsed, tough stems removed

1/4 pound fresh spinach, well rinsed and tough stems removed, sliced into fine shreds

Minced parsley, for garnish

*S*everal hours before serving, prepare tomato sauce. In a small saucepan, combine tomatoes, onion, garlic, oil, lemon juice, salt, pepper and sugar. Heat through to a simmer, then remove from heat and set aside (do not refrigerate).

*O*ne and a half hours before serving, lay chicken breasts in a shallow dish and marinate in olive oil, lemon juice and rosemary mixture.

*T*oss romaine lettuce and watercress together; wrap in paper toweling and refrigerate until needed. Refrigerate shredded spinach until needed.

*S*hortly before serving time, line 6 dinner-size plates with the romaine and watercress and top with about 1/4 cup tomato sauce.

*P*reheat broiler, drain chicken breasts, place on broiler pan and broil 3 inches from heat for about 4 to 5 minutes; do not overcook. Chicken can also be grilled over hot coals, about 2 minutes on each side. Remove from broiler with tongs and place on top of greens on each plate. Place equal amounts of shredded spinach on top of each chicken breast and top each with remaining tomato sauce. Sprinkle with parsley and serve immediately.

*S*erves 6.

# Chicken and Summer Fruit Salad

*Perfect for a hot summer night. Cheese and Chili Pepper Biscuits provide an interesting contrast.*

6 boneless, skinless chicken breasts

2 cups chicken broth

1/2 teaspoon salt

1 teaspoon thyme

1 small very ripe cantaloupe, skin removed and thinly sliced

3 nectarines, thinly sliced and sprinkled with lemon juice

1 cup mayonnaise

1 tablespoon honey

3 tablespoons broth or more to thin dressing

1 tablespoon grated orange peel

2 tablespoons sliced almonds, for garnish

Several hours or the day before serving, add chicken broth, salt and thyme to a large skillet and bring to a boil. Reduce heat, add chicken breasts and barely simmer for 15 minutes. Remove from heat and cool chicken breasts in the broth. Remove chicken, cover with plastic wrap and refrigerate until ready to slice. Over high heat, reduce broth until only a few tablespoons remain. Strain and reserve.

In a small bowl, mix together mayonnaise, honey, broth and orange peel; set aside or refrigerate until serving time.

Shortly before serving, thinly slice chilled chicken breasts and arrange down center of large platter. Arrange the sliced fruit attractively around the chicken, spoon a ribbon of dressing over the chicken and fruit and sprinkle with almonds.

Serves 6.

# Pineapple, Orange and Chicken Salad

*The fruits complement the chicken so nicely and the chow mein noodles add a surprising crunch.*

15-ounce can pineapple chunks, packed in natural juice

2 navel oranges, peeled and white pith removed, broken into segments (if very large cut in half)

4 cups cooked, cubed chicken

1/2 cup thinly sliced celery

1/2 cup chopped sweet green pepper

3 green onions, thinly sliced

1 cup mayonnaise

1 tablespoon Dijon-style mustard

1 tablespoon orange juice

2 teaspoons grated orange peel

5-ounce can chow mein noodles, slightly broken

Boston or bibb lettuce, for lining salad bowl

In a large bowl, combine pineapple cubes, orange segments, chicken cubes, celery, pepper and onions. Set aside.

In a small bowl, mix mayonnaise, mustard, orange juice and orange peel. Pour over the salad, mix thoroughly and refrigerate several hours or overnight.

Line a large bowl, preferably glass, with lettuce and mound the salad in the bowl; sprinkle with noodles. Serve immediately.

Serves 6.

# Chicken and Pasta Twists with a Spicy Sauce

*This is a variation of a favorite salad from our first book, THE PASTA SALAD BOOK.*

4 boneless chicken breasts, poached, skin removed and meat torn into shreds

8 ounces pasta twists

1 tablespoon sesame or salad oil

1/4 pound snow peas, tipped and strings removed, then cooked 3 minutes, drained and chilled (or 1/2 box frozen snow peas, thawed)

6 canned water chestnuts, halved and thinly sliced

4 green onions, sliced diagonally in 1/2-inch pieces

2 tablespoons toasted sesame seeds

6 tablespoons creamy peanut butter

1-inch piece ginger root, minced

2 garlic cloves, minced

5 tablespoons soy sauce

2 tablespoons red wine vinegar

2 tablespoons sesame oil

1 teaspoon hot chili oil, or more to taste

1/2 teaspoon ground Szechuan peppercorns

2 tablespoons warm water, approximately

Cook pasta until al dente, drain, rinse with cold water and drain again. Toss with 1 tablespoon sesame or salad oil.

Combine in a large bowl pasta, chicken, snow peas, water chestnuts, onions and sesame seeds.

Add to food processor bowl or blender peanut butter, ginger root, garlic, soy sauce, vinegar, sesame oil, chili oil, peppercorns and water. Whirl until smooth. Pour over salad and toss thoroughly. Refrigerate for at least 2 hours so flavors can blend. Toss before serving and taste for seasonings. Serve lightly chilled.

Serves 6.

# Oriental-Style Chicken Salad with Greens and Mushrooms

*Try this salad with sweet corn on the cob and Herbed Pita Triangles.*

6 chicken breast halves

1/4 cup melted butter

Salt, pepper and garlic powder

1/2 pound mushrooms, thinly sliced

3 Belgian endives, trimmed, halved crosswise, and leaves separated

1 bunch watercress, tough stems removed

1 head Boston lettuce, torn into small pieces

1/2 cup minced green onions

1/4 cup chopped fresh tarragon or basil

2-inch piece ginger root, halved and cut into slivers

2 tablespoons toasted sesame seeds

1/4 cup salad oil

1/4 cup sesame oil

3 tablespoons white wine vinegar

1 tablespoon dry sherry

1/4 cup soy sauce

1 tablespoon Dijon-style mustard

1/2 teaspoon salt, or more to taste

1/4 teaspoon crushed red pepper

Brush chicken breasts with melted butter and sprinkle with salt, pepper and garlic powder to taste. Arrange skin side down on the rack of a broiler pan and place pan so that chicken is about 5 inches from heat source. Broil 10 to 12 minutes, turn and broil about 5 minutes. Cool, remove skin and bones and tear meat into shreds. Toss chicken with 1/2 cup dressing and set aside while preparing vegetables.

Whisk together in a small bowl the salad oil, sesame oil, vinegar, sherry, soy sauce, mustard, salt and crushed red pepper.

Toss together in a large bowl the mushrooms, Belgium endive, watercress, Boston lettuce, green onions, tarragon and sesame seeds. Add remaining dressing and toss to coat. Transfer vegetables to a platter or large bowl and top with the prepared chicken. Serve salad at room temperature or lightly chilled.

Serves 6.

# Sauteed Chicken Livers on Fresh Spinach

*This rather unusual combination of ingredients and the hot and cold sensations will intrigue your guests. Serve with a good French bread to dab in the tasty sauce.*

1 pound fresh spinach, thoroughly washed and heavy stems removed, torn into smaller pieces

1/2 pound mushrooms, thinly sliced

4 hard-cooked eggs, chopped

6 green onions, sliced into 1/2-inch pieces

1 pound chicken livers, halved

1/2 cup flour

1 teaspoon salt

1/4 teaspoon pepper

1/2 teaspoon powdered poultry seasoning

1 tablespoon salad oil

3 tablespoons butter

1/2 cup whipping cream

1/4 cup salad oil

Juice of 1 lemon

2 tablespoons herb or white wine vinegar

2 green onions, white part only, finely minced

1 garlic clove, minced

1/2 teaspoon tarragon or basil, crushed

1/2 teaspoon salt, or more to taste

1/4 teaspoon freshly ground pepper

*T*oss together in a large bowl spinach, mushrooms, eggs and onions. Cover with plastic wrap and refrigerate for several hours or while preparing sauce and chicken livers.

*I*n a small bowl, mix together whipping cream, oil, lemon juice, vinegar, onions, garlic, tarragon, salt and pepper.

*S*hortly before serving, arrange salad mixture on 6 dinner-sized plates; set aside while preparing chicken livers.

*A*dd flour, salt, pepper and poultry seasoning to a paper bag. Add small amounts of livers to bag and shake to coat. Heat oil and butter in a large skillet over medium heat, add floured livers and saute until browned but still pink inside. Remove to a bowl and cover to keep warm.

*A*dd 1/2 cup sauce to skillet and quickly deglaze pan; pour sauce over sauteed chicken livers. Place an equal amount of livers in the center of each salad and drizzle the remaining sauce over the salad. Serve immediately.

*S*erves 6.

# Turkey and Rice Salad
# with Ginger Dressing

*Of course left-over turkey is ideal, but you could also cook a turkey breast just for this terrific salad.*

1 cup long-grain rice, cooked to package directions and cooled

2-3 cups shredded cooked turkey

1 cup frozen tiny peas, thawed and blanched with boiling water

1/2 cup chopped green onions

1/2 cup coarsely grated carrots

1/2 cup chopped sweet red or green pepper

1/4 cup toasted sliced almonds

3/4 cup salad oil

1/4 cup lemon juice

1 tablespoons vinegar, or more to taste

1/4 cup soy sauce

2 garlic cloves, minced

1 teaspoon minced ginger root

1/2 teaspoon salt

1/4 teaspoon hot pepper sauce

*In* a large salad bowl, combine cooked rice, turkey, peas, onions, carrots, peppers and almonds.

*In* a small bowl, whisk together salad oil, lemon juice, vinegar, soy sauce, garlic, ginger, pepper sauce and salt. Pour 1 cup dressing over salad ingredients and mix thoroughly. Refrigerate for several hours or overnight. Before serving, toss salad, taste for seasoning and add remaining dressing as needed.

*S*erves 6.

# Turkey Salad Nicoise

*There is no reason, of course, why you couldn't substitute roast chicken for the turkey and enjoy this salad just as much.*

3 cups shredded or cubed cooked turkey

1/2 pound green beans, trimmed, halved and cooked for 5 minutes in simmering, salted water

4 medium potatoes, cooked, peeled and diced

3 medium tomatoes, cut in wedges

3 hard-cooked eggs, quartered

18 black olives, preferably small Nicoise olives

Boston or bibb lettuce to line plates

1/2 cup chopped parsley, for garnish

1/4 cup capers, for garnish

1/2 of a 2-ounce tin anchovy fillets, drained and chopped

3 tablespoons red wine vinegar

2 teaspoons Dijon-style mustard

1 garlic clove, minced

1/4 teaspoon freshly ground pepper

2/3 cup extra-virgin olive oil

Salt to taste

*I*n a small bowl, mash the anchovies with the vinegar, mustard, garlic and pepper. Whisk in the oil and taste for salt. Mix 1/2 cup dressing with the turkey and set aside.

*L*ine 6 dinner-size plates with lettuce and place a serving of the turkey in the center of the lettuce. Divide the beans, potatoes, tomatoes, eggs and olives among the plates and drizzle with the remaining dressing. Scatter each salad with parsley and capers. Serve at room temperature or lightly chilled.

*A*n alternative to arranging the salad on individual plates is to line a large platter with the lettuce and arrange all the salad ingredients attractively on the lettuce, then drizzle with dressing and garnish with parsley and capers.

*S*erves 6.

# Curried Turkey Salad

*This is a variation of a hot curry entree that we are all more familiar with. Your family or guests will enjoy selecting their own garnishes for the salad.*

3 cups shredded or diced cooked turkey

2 large stalks celery, thinly sliced

1/2 cup chopped sweet green pepper

1/2 cup slivered almonds, toasted

1/2 cup golden raisins

1/4 cup thinly sliced green onions

1/4 cup chopped mango chutney

*Garnishes:*
Hard-cooked eggs quartered

Chopped mango chutney

Crisp-cooked green beans, quartered

Crisp-cooked sliced carrots

Cucumber slices

Melon balls

Orange segments, halved or quartered

Shredded iceberg lettuce to line salad bowl

1 cup mayonnaise

1-1/2 tablespoons curry powder, or more to taste

1 tablespoon Dijon-style mustard

1 tablespoon lemon juice

2 garlic cloves, minced

Milk to thin dressing

*I*n a small bowl, mix together mayonnaise, curry powder, mustard, lemon juice, garlic and 1 tablespoon milk.

*I*n a large bowl, combine turkey, celery, pepper, raisins, almonds, onions and chutney. Add 1/2 cup curried mayonnaise and mix thoroughly. Cover and refrigerate for several hours or overnight.

*A*t serving time, line a bowl with lettuce leaves and add turkey salad. Arrange garnishes in separate bowls and plates, and place on table. Thin the remaining curried mayonnaise with milk to a pouring consistency; pass separately for pouring over the selected garnishes on each plate.

*S*erves 6.

# Curried Turkey Salad in Cantaloupe Halves

*This is a pretty as well as tasty salad, but it should only be served when sweet ripe cantaloupes are available.*

3 cups shredded or diced cooked turkey

1 cup thinly sliced celery

1/2 cup chopped sweet red pepper

1/2 cup minced green onions

1/2 cup golden raisins

4-6 slices bacon, fried crisply and crumbled

3 cantaloupes, halved and seeded

2/3 cup mayonnaise

1/3 cup chopped mango chutney, or more to taste

2 teaspoons curry powder, or more to taste

1/4 teaspoon salt

1/4 teaspoon freshly ground pepper

1/2 cup chopped honey-roasted peanuts, for garnish

*In* a small bowl, mix together mayonnaise, chutney, curry powder, salt and pepper.

*In* a large bowl, combine turkey, celery, pepper, onions, raisins and bacon. Add curried mayonnaise and mix thoroughly. Divide turkey salad among the cantaloupe halves and sprinkle each with chopped peanuts. Serve immediately or lightly chilled.

*S*erves 6.

# Salads with Meat

# Salads with Meat

*B*its *of last night's leg of lamb, spicy sausages sliced into bite-sized pieces, half a steak grilled rare—all turned into hearty main-course meals to delight the palate and pamper the budget. In fact, we suggest you plan on cooking a little extra meat to turn into one of these salads the next night.*

# Composed Vegetable and Meat Salad with Onion Vinaigrette

*The "do-ahead" possibilities of this salad will leave time to whip up an easy Parsley Pepper Bread to serve with it.*

2 medium zucchini, scrubbed and cut into 2-inch julienne strips

2 medium carrots, scraped and cut into 2-inch julienne strips

1 red sweet pepper, halved lengthwise and cut into thin crescents

1 green sweet pepper, halved lengthwise and cut into thin crescents

1 pound smoked tongue, thickly sliced and diced

1/2 pound sliced hard salami, cut into 1/2-inch pieces

1/2 pound Swiss or Gruyere cheese, cut into 1/2-inch dice

6 strips crisply fried bacon, crumbled

1 cup extra-virgin olive oil

1/3 cup fresh lemon juice

1 tablespoon Dijon-style mustard

1/4 cup minced green onion, tops only

1/2 teaspoon thyme

1/2 teaspoon salt, or more to taste

1/4 teaspoon freshly ground pepper

4 cups iceberg and romaine lettuce, sliced 1/4-inch wide, to line plates

1/2 cup Nicoise or other cured black olives, for garnish

As you prepare each vegetable, meat and cheese, place it in a separate bowl and cover with plastic wrap; refrigerate if preparing before serving time.

In a small bowl, whisk together olive oil, lemon juice, mustard, green onion tops, thyme, salt and pepper. Set aside but do not refrigerate.

Shortly before serving, pour a small amount of dressing over each of the prepared vegetables, meats and cheese and mix to coat. Divide the iceberg and romaine lettuce among 6 dinner-size plates. Arrange the salad ingredients attractively on each plate and garnish with the Nicoise olives and crumbled bacon. Pass the remaining dressing separately.

Serves 6.

# Deli Chef's Salad

*What could be easier than stopping at the deli counter for the main ingredients of this salad, then adding a crunchy bread from the bakery section. Ask the deli person to slice the meats and cheese slightly thicker than usual.*

1/3 pound sliced turkey breast, cut into julienne strips

1/3 pound sliced roast beef, cut into julienne strips

1/3 pound sliced baked ham, cut into julienne strips

1/3 pound Swiss cheese, cut into 1/2-inch squares

1/2 cup thinly sliced red onion

1 green sweet pepper, thinly sliced

1 small jar marinated artichokes, drained and halved

5 cups torn mixed greens

1 cup herbed croutons, preferably homemade

3/4 cup virgin olive oil

3 tablespoons red wine vinegar

1 tablespoon tomato paste

2 teaspoons prepared mustard

1/2 teaspoon paprika, or more to taste

1/2 teaspoon salt

1/4 teaspoon freshly ground pepper

4 hard-cooked eggs, quartered, for garnish

3 medium tomatoes, quartered, for garnish

*I*n a small bowl, whisk together the olive oil, vinegar, tomato paste, mustard, paprika, salt and pepper.

*I*n a medium bowl, combine the sliced deli meats, cheese and onion slices. Pour 1/2 cup dressing in the bowl and toss. Cover and refrigerate for at least 2 hours.

*A*t serving time, place the mixed greens, sliced pepper and artichoke hearts in a large shallow bowl and toss with 1/2 cup dressing. Drain the marinated mixture (add the marinade to any remaining dressing) and mound in the center of the bowl. Garnish with the quartered eggs and tomatoes and sprinkle with the croutons. Pass the remaining dressing in a small bowl.

*S*erves 6.

# Spicy Paté Salad

*This rather elegant salad is not nearly as time-consuming as your guests or family might think: just purchase the paté from the gourmet food store.*

1/2 pound spicy paté, sliced and cut into narrow, 2-inch long strips

1 pound green beans, cut into 2-inch pieces and cooked just until crisp

2 medium red-skinned apples, unpeeled

Juice of 1/2 lemon

1/2 cup extra-virgin olive oil

1/4 cup lemon juice

1/4 cup chopped pecans

1/4 cup chopped green onions

1 teaspoon dry mustard

1 teaspoon grated lemon peel

1/2 teaspoon salt, or more to taste

1/4 teaspoon freshly ground pepper

1/3 cup chopped, toasted pecans, for garnish

Boston or bibb lettuce leaves to line platter

*P*lace the oil, lemon juice, pecans, onions, dry mustard, lemon peel, salt and pepper in a food processor bowl or blender and mix until smooth. Transfer to a medium bowl, add the green beans and toss to coat. Cover and refrigerate for several hours or overnight. Remove from the refrigerator 1 hour before serving.

*S*hortly before serving, core and julienne the apples and toss with lemon juice to prevent browning. Set aside.

*L*ine a large platter with the lettuce leaves and arrange green beans in center, surround with julienne apples, and arrange paté strips over beans. Sprinkle salad with toasted pecans.

*S*erves 6.

# Green Beans, Ham, and Gruyere with Walnut-Dill Dressing

*This is a wonderful summer supper salad to serve when green beans are at their peak.*

1-1/2 pounds green beans, trimmed and cut in half

1 cup diced smoked ham

1/2 cup diced Gruyere cheese

1/2 cup thinly sliced green onions

1/2 red sweet pepper, thinly sliced

1/2 cup olive oil

1/3 cup walnut oil, available in large supermarkets or specialty food stores

1/3 cup red wine vinegar

1/2 cup fresh dillweed (do not use dried dill)

1/4 cup sliced green onions

1/4 cup coarsely chopped parsley

1/4 cup coarsely chopped walnuts

1/2 teaspoon salt, or more to taste

1/4 teaspoon freshly ground pepper, or more to taste

6 hard-cooked eggs, quartered, for garnish

*A*dd beans to boiling salted water, reduce heat and simmer about 5 minutes or until barely tender. Drain in a colander, rinse with cold water and drain thoroughly before adding to a large salad bowl. When beans are cool, add ham, cheese, green onions and red pepper. Cover with plastic wrap and refrigerate while preparing dressing.

*A*dd to a food processor or blender the olive oil, walnut oil, vinegar, dillweed, green onions, parsley, walnuts, salt and pepper. Process until almost smooth. Taste for seasoning and adjust to taste.

*A*dd 1/2 cup dressing to salad ingredients and mix to coat. Arrange quartered eggs around the salad and pass the remaining dressing in a small sauceboat.

*S*erves 6.

# Maine Ham, Fontina Cheese and Cabbage Salad

*This easy salad originated during our first vacation in Maine; it's been a summer treat ever since.*

3/4 pound boiled ham, julienned into 1-1/2 x 1/4-inch pieces (ask the deli-person to slice the ham thicker than usual)

1/2 pound Fontina cheese, julienned into 1 x 1/4-inch pieces

2 cups coarsely shredded cabbage

1/4 cup minced red onion

1/4 cup minced parsley

3/4 cup olive oil

1/4 cup red wine vinegar

1 tablespoon Dijon-style mustard

1 clove garlic, minced

1/4 teaspoon freshly ground pepper

1/4 cup crumbled Roquefort cheese

Salt to taste

Boston lettuce to line shallow bowl or platter

6 large mushrooms, cleaned and diced, for garnish

2 hard-cooked eggs, chopped, for garnish

*In* a large bowl, combine the ham, Fontina cheese, cabbage, red onion and parsley. Cover with plastic wrap and refrigerate while preparing dressing.

*In* a small bowl, whisk together the oil, vinegar, mustard, garlic and pepper. With a fork, stir in the Roquefort cheese until dressing is almost smooth. Taste for salt and adjust to taste. Add the dressing to the salad ingredients and mix thoroughly. Line a shallow bowl or platter with the lettuce leaves and mound the salad in the center. Garnish with the diced mushrooms and chopped eggs. Serve lightly chilled.

*S*erves 6.

# Ham and Rutabaga Salad

*Did you know that the rutabaga is a member of the cabbage family and that Thomas Jefferson introduced it to America?*

1-1/2 pounds sliced smoked ham, cut into 2 x 1/2-inch strips

1 large rutabaga, peeled and sliced 1/4-inch thick, then cut into thin strips

1/2 bunch watercress, tough stems removed and coarsely chopped

3/4 cup mayonnaise

1 tablespoon olive oil

1 tablespoon lemon juice

2 teaspoons Worcestershire sauce

2 teaspoons fresh minced dillweed or 1 teaspoon dried

1/2 teaspoon salt

1/4 teaspoon freshly ground pepper

Shredded iceberg lettuce to line salad bowl

2 tablespoons chopped walnuts

1 tablespoon snipped fresh dill, for garnish (if not available use 2 tablespoons minced parsley)

*I*n a large bowl, combine the ham, rutabaga and watercress. In a small bowl, mix together the mayonnaise, olive oil, lemon juice, Worcestershire sauce, dillweed, salt and pepper. Add to the salad ingredients and mix thoroughly.

*L*ine a salad bowl with the shredded lettuce, fill with the salad, and garnish with chopped walnuts and dill or parsley. Serve well chilled.

*S*erves 6.

# Picnic Potato, Ham, Cabbage and Cheese Salad

*E*xcept *for the potato chips and devil's food cake, you have the fixings for a picnic all in one bowl with this salad.*

2-1/2 pounds red-skin or new potatoes, cooked and cut into 1-inch cubes

1 pound baked ham, sliced thickly and cut into narrow strips

2 cups coarsely shredded cabbage

2 cups Swiss cheese, coarsely grated

1/2 cup chopped dill pickles

1/4 cup minced onion

1/4 cup chopped parsley

2/3 cup olive oil

1/4 cup white wine vinegar

2 tablespoons Dijon-style mustard

1 teaspoon dillweed, or more to taste

1 teaspoon thyme

1 teaspoon salt, or more to taste

1/2 teaspoon freshly ground pepper

1/4 cup minced parsley, for garnish

*W*hile potatoes are cooking, whisk in a small bowl the olive oil, vinegar, mustard, dillweed, thyme, salt and pepper; set aside. After potatoes have cooled and been cut into cubes (they do not have to be peeled, just well scrubbed before cooking), put them into a large bowl and mix them with 1/2 cup dressing. Cool to room temperature.

*A*dd to the cooled potatoes the ham, cabbage, cheese, pickles and parsley, and toss. Add the remaining dressing, mix again and chill lightly. Taste for seasoning and adjust if necessary. Garnish with minced parsley before serving.

*S*alad can be prepared the day before but remove from the refrigerator 1 hour before serving; taste for seasoning and adjust.

*S*erves 6.

# Ham Salad in a Puff Bowl

*The easily prepared Puff Bowl adds a touch of the exotic to this tasty ham salad.*

Puff Bowl (see page 21)

2 cups cubed cooked ham

10 ounce package frozen tiny peas, thawed and blanched with boiling water, then drained

1-1/2 cups shredded Cheddar cheese

8-ounce can pineapple chunks, well drained

1/2 cup coarsely chopped pecans

2/3 cup mayonnaise

2 tablespoons minced onion

1 tablespoon lemon juice

1/2 teaspoon sugar

1/2 teaspoon salt

1/2 teaspoon dry mustard

2 cups shredded iceberg lettuce to line Puff Bowl

1/4 cup toasted shredded coconut, for garnish

*P*repare Puff Bowl as directed.

*C*ombine in a large bowl the ham, peas, Cheddar cheese, pineapple chunks and pecans.

*M*ix together in a small bowl the mayonnaise, onion, lemon juice, sugar, salt and dry mustard. Pour over the salad and mix gently but thoroughly. Cover with plastic wrap and refrigerate up to several hours if not using immediately.

*S*hortly before serving, place the Puff Bowl on an attractive round plate, scatter the lettuce on the bottom and fill with the ham salad. Sprinkle with coconut and present at the table before slicing.

*S*erves 6.

# St. Remy Vegetable and Bacon Salad

*If you close your eyes while eating this salad you might think you're in a bistro in Provence. Serve with a crunchy baguette and a glass of your favorite red wine.*

1/2 pound slab bacon, cut into 1 x 2-inch cubes

3 large red-skinned potatoes, cooked and diced (do not peel)

2 bulbs fennel, trimmed, quartered and sliced 1/4-inch thick (if not available substitute 3 small turnips, peeled, quartered and thinly sliced)

1 large onion, quartered and thinly sliced

1 large head escarole, rinsed, tough leaves discarded and the remainder torn into small pieces

1 cup tiny frozen peas, thawed and blanched with boiling water and well drained

3 tablespoons red wine vinegar

2 teaspoons Dijon-style mustard

2/3 cup olive oil

1 teaspoon Provencal herbs (or equal parts thyme, rosemary and basil)

1/2 teaspoon salt, or more to taste

1/4 teaspoon freshly ground pepper, or more to taste

1 clove garlic, halved

1/2 cup croutons, preferably homemade

1/4 cup chopped parsley, for garnish

In a large skillet, fry the cubed bacon until golden but not crisp and hard; remove with a slotted spoon and drain on paper toweling. Add the diced potatoes to the hot bacon fat and toss and fry until golden on all sides; remove with a slotted spoon to a bowl. Add the sliced fennel or turnips to the fat and fry until slightly soft and golden; add to the bowl with the potatoes. Add onions and fry until limp and golden, but not brown; add to the other vegetables and sprinkle lightly with salt. Keep warm while preparing dressing and salad bowl.

Add the vinegar to the hot bacon fat and scrape up any browned bits from the bottom of the skillet. Add the mustard, then whisk in the salad oil, herbs, salt and pepper. Keep dressing on a very low heat while preparing salad bowl.

Rub a large glass or pottery bowl with the garlic halves (discard garlic), then add bacon, fried vegetables, escarole, peas, croutons and dressing and toss gently to coat. Sprinkle with chopped parsley and serve immediately.

Serves 6.

# Yin and Yang Pork Tenderloin Salad

*This is another salad of hot and cold contrasts that is tasty and fun to eat.*

1-1/2 pounds boneless pork tenderloin, cut into 1/2-inch cubes

3 tablespoons soy sauce

1 tablespoon water

1 tablespoon white wine

1 tablespoon vinegar

2 teaspoons sesame oil

1/2 cup salad oil

1 medium onion coarsely chopped

1 tablespoon minced garlic

2 cups sliced iceberg lettuce

3 large carrots, peeled and coarsely grated

2 cucumbers, quartered lengthwise, seeded and diced

1/2 cup sweet bean paste, available in large supermarkets or Oriental food stores

6 tablespoons soy sauce

1 tablespoon white wine

2 teaspoons sugar

12 ounces Chinese egg noodles or thin spaghetti

1 tablespoon each, salad oil and sesame oil

*M*arinate the pork cubes for 30 minutes in 3 tablespoons soy sauce, water, white wine, corn starch and sesame oil. Mix together bean paste, remaining soy sauce, white wine and sugar and set aside.

*B*ring about 3 quarts salted water to a boil and cook the egg noodles until al dente. Drain well, transfer to a large bowl and mix with 1 tablespoon each salad oil and sesame oil. Cover with plastic wrap while stir-frying pork cubes.

*H*eat a wok or large skillet until very hot, then add the 1/2 cup salad oil. When oil is hot, add the pork cubes and marinade and stir-fry 3 to 4 minutes. Transfer with a slotted spoon to a bowl.

*A*dd the onion to the hot oil and fry until the onion is golden; add the garlic and bean paste mixture and cook about 2 minutes. Pour the sauce over the pork and toss together. Add the meat to the noodles and surround with the lettuce, carrots and cucumbers. Serve immediately and toss lightly at the table.

*S*erves 6.

# Antipasto Salad in Lettuce Cups

*A*dd *a loaf of crunchy Italian bread or dense Foccacio flat bread and a bottle of vino and you will think you're in Tuscany.*

2 large red sweet peppers, roasted

1/2 pound provolone cheese, coarsely grated

1/2 pound prosciutto or peppered beef from the deli, cut into thin strips

1 cup canned garbanzo beans (or chickpeas) marinated in 1/2 cup dressing for at least 30 minutes

12 large green olives

3/4 cup extra-virgin olive oil

3 tablespoons red wine vinegar

1/2 tin anchovy fillets, mashed

1 tablespoon fresh basil, minced, or 1 teaspoon dried, crushed

1 garlic clove, minced

1/4 teaspoon freshly ground pepper

Salt to taste

12 large radicchio leaves or red lettuce leaves

Fresh basil leaves, for garnish

Grated Parmesan cheese, for garnish

*P*lace peppers on the oven rack 4 inches below a preheated broiler. Turn with tongs to char evenly; this will take about 10 minutes. Place in a paper bag, close tightly and set aside to cool. Remove from the bag and rinse off the charred skin under cold running water. Core and seed the peppers, slice thinly, set aside.

*W*hisk together the olive oil, vinegar, anchovy fillets, basil, garlic and pepper; taste for salt. Pour 1/2 cup dressing over beans. Arrange radicchio or lettuce leaves on 6 salad plates. Divide roasted peppers, provolone, prosciutto, beans and olives among the plates. Drizzle with the remaining dressing and garnish with the basil leaves. Pass the grated Parmesan cheese.

*S*erves 6.

# Rice with Spicy Sausage and Oranges

*This salad has a definite Latin flavor as well as a good contrast of colors and texture.*

3 cups cooked long-grain rice, at room temperature

1/2 pound chorizo sausage, cut in half lengthwise, then sliced thinly (cooked hot Italian sausage or kielbasa can be used if chorizo is unavailable)

3 large oranges, peeled, white pith removed, then diced

10-ounce box frozen corn, thawed, blanched with boiling water and drained well

4 green onions, chopped

1/2 cup canned black beans, well drained

1/2 cup chopped cilantro or parsley

1/2 cup olive oil, divided

3 tablespoons lemon juice

2 teaspoons grated orange zest

1/2 teaspoon salt

1/8 teaspoon Tabasco sauce

1/4 cup toasted slivered almonds, for garnish

Shredded iceberg lettuce to serve with the salad

Add 2 tablespoons oil to a medium skillet and lightly brown the sausage. Transfer to a paper towel and drain; cool. In a large pottery bowl, combine the rice, sausage, oranges, corn, onions, black beans and cilantro.

Whisk together in a small bowl the remaining olive oil, lemon juice, orange rind, salt and Tabasco sauce. Pour over the salad and mix thoroughly. Taste for seasoning and adjust to taste. Sprinkle with almonds and serve with shredded lettuce.

Serves 6.

# Brunch-Time Scrambled Egg and Sausage Salad

*This would be especially nice to serve on a warm summer morning. The eggs can be scrambled and the sausage browned before your guests arrive.*

8 eggs

3 tablespoons table cream

1/2 teaspoon salt

2 tablespoons butter

1/2 pound crisply cooked and drained bulk country sausage

1 cup seeded and chopped tomatoes

6 green onions, chopped

3 tablespoons olive oil

1 tablespoon lemon juice

1 teaspoon prepared mustard

3 tablespoons minced parsley

Whisk together the eggs, cream and salt. Melt the butter in large skillet over medium-low heat. Pour in the egg mixture and cook until set, using a spoon to keep the eggs in motion so they don't get crusty on the bottom. Remove to a bowl to cool. Chop into small pieces when cool.

Add the chopped tomatoes and onions to an appropriate size bowl. Pour the olive oil and lemon juice over the vegetables and toss lightly. Add the chopped eggs and crisp sausage and toss again. Sprinkle with minced parsley and serve.

Serves 6.

# Smoked Sausage, Bean and Beet Salad

*This is a hearty "old world" salad that a dense rye bread or the Caraway Biscuits and a bottle of cold beer would complement very nicely.*

1 pound kielbasa or other smoked link sausage

3 cups cooked white beans (canned or cooked dried, rinsed and drained)

8-ounce can sliced beets, drained and slices quartered

1 cup chopped dill pickles

1/2 cup chopped green onions

1/2 cup olive oil

3 tablespoons red wine vinegar

2 teaspoons prepared mustard

1 teaspoon horseradish

1/2 teaspoon thyme

1/2 teaspoon salt

1/4 teaspoon freshly ground pepper

2 cups shredded iceberg lettuce, for garnish

1/4 cup chopped parsley, for garnish

*P*lace sausage in a large skillet and almost cover with water. Bring to a simmer and cook about 10 minutes, just to heat through. Remove to a cutting board and slice lengthwise, then in 1/2-inch widths.

*I*n a large bowl, combine the sausage, beans, beets, pickles and onions.

*W*hisk together in a small bowl the olive oil, vinegar, mustard, horseradish, thyme, salt and pepper. Pour the dressing over the salad ingredients and mix well. Cover with plastic wrap and chill slightly. Or prepare early in the day and refrigerate but bring to almost room temperature before serving.

*T*ransfer to a shallow bowl and garnish outer edge of salad with shredded lettuce and sprinkle with chopped parsley.

*S*erves 6.

# Double Bean and Sausage Salad

*A hearty winter salad that's great on a buffet table or to nosh after the big game.*

4 cups warm kidney beans, drained
4 cups warm navy or pea beans, drained
1 pound smoked Polish sausage
1 cup thinly sliced celery
1/2 cup thinly sliced green onions
1/2 cup chopped sweet green pepper
1/2 cup chopped sweet red pepper
1/4 cup chopped parsley
1/2 teaspoon marjoram
2/3 cup olive oil
3 tablespoons vinegar
1 tablespoon prepared mustard
1/2 teaspoon salt, or more to taste
1/4 teaspoon freshly ground pepper
1 garlic clove, minced
4 hard-cooked eggs, sliced
1/4 cup minced parsley

*P*lace sausage in a large skillet and almost cover with water. Bring to a simmer and cook about 10 minutes, just to heat through. Remove to a cutting board and slice in 1/4-inch thick pieces. Combine warm sausage with warm beans in a large bowl. Add celery, onions, green and red peppers, parsley and marjoram and mix together.

*I*n a small bowl, whisk together the olive oil, vinegar, mustard, salt, pepper and garlic. Pour the dressing over the salad and mix thoroughly. Transfer salad to a large bowl or platter. Arrange egg slices attractively around salad and sprinkle salad with minced parsley. Serve salad warm or at room temperature.

*S*erves 6.

# Muffuletta (Olive, Sausage and Cheese Salad-Sandwich)

*This is a variation of the classic New Orleans specialty that can be found in all manner of restaurants in that unique city.*

1 good quality Italian or sourdough bread

1-1/2 cups chopped pimento-stuffed olives

1 cup Greek or other cured black olives, pitted and chopped

1 cup olive oil

1/2 cup chopped parsley

1-ounce tin anchovy fillets, chopped

2 tablespoons capers, drained

2 teaspoons minced garlic

1/2 teaspoon freshly ground pepper

1/2 large head iceberg lettuce, thinly sliced

1/4 pound thinly sliced Genoa salami

1/4 pound thinly sliced mortadella or bologna

1/3 pound thinly sliced Provolone cheese

*T*wenty-four hours before serving, add the oil, parsley, anchovy fillets, capers, garlic and pepper to the bowl of a food processor or blender and mix until almost smooth. Combine with the olives in a medium-size bowl and refrigerate.

*A*ssemble the salad 2 hours before serving. Drain the marinated chopped olives and reserve the dressing. Slice the top third off the bread and remove most of the bread, leaving a 1/2-inch shell.

*G*enerously brush both shells with the reserved dressing. Spread some of the lettuce on the bottom shell. Spread lettuce with half of the marinated olive mixture. Divide the salami, mortadella and cheese so that you have 2 alternating layers of each in the bottom part of the bread. Spread some of the lettuce between each layer and sprinkle lightly with remaining dressing. Spread with the remaining olive mixture, then cover with the top bread shell. Wrap the bread tightly in foil, place on a platter, then weigh down with about a 5-pound weight for no less than 1 hour.

*A*t serving time, remove wrapping and slice at least 1-inch thick.

*S*erves 6.

# Curly Endive and Kielbasa Salad

*On a cold winter night, serve this warm salad with steaming bowls of bean soup and buttered black bread.*

1 head curly endive, washed and torn into small pieces

1 pound all beef kielbasa, cut into small dice

1 small onion, finely chopped

1 garlic clove, minced

3 tablespoons red wine vinegar

4 tablespoons olive oil

1/2 teaspoon salt

1/4 teaspoon freshly ground pepper, or more to taste

1/2 cup finely diced sweet red pepper

1/2 cup small croutons, preferably homemade

Shake as much water from the endive as possible, then place in a large salad bowl. Cover with plastic wrap and refrigerate.

Shortly before serving, saute the diced kielbasa in a large skillet over medium high heat. Toss and stir until all sides are nicely browned and crisp. Remove with a slotted spoon to a plate lined with paper towels, and cover with foil to keep warm.

Add chopped onion and garlic to pan and saute until almost soft. Off the heat, add the vinegar and scrape up all the browned bits in the pan. Add the oil, salt and pepper and return to a low heat to warm through.

To the endive in the salad bowl add the warm kielbasa, the peppers and croutons. Toss lightly, then pour the warm dressing over and toss again. Serve immediately.

Serves 6.

# Salad from Bologna

*We tried to recreate this simple salad that we enjoyed at a trattoria near the university in Bologna. Add a good Italian bread and a recording of a Puccini opera, and spirit yourself away.*

6 medium potatoes, peeled, halved lengthwise and thinly sliced

1/3 cup herb or white wine vinegar

1 tablespoon extra-virgin olive oil

1 teaspoon rosemary, crushed

1 pound thickly sliced mortadella (or bologna), cut into 1-inch squares

1/2 pound sliced provolone cheese, cut into 1-1/2 x 1-inch strips

1/2 cup minced red onion

1/4 cup chopped parsley, preferably the flat-leaf variety

2 tablespoons capers, drained

1/2 cup extra-virgin olive oil

3 tablespoons herb or white wine vinegar

1 tablespoon country-style mustard, or more to taste

1 garlic clove, minced

1/2 teaspoon salt, or more to taste

1/4 teaspoon freshly ground pepper

Arugula leaves or Romaine lettuce, for garnish

*C*ook potato slices in a large saucepan of boiling salted water for about 5 minutes, or until barely tender. Drain in a colander and transfer to a large bowl. Gently mix in 1/3 cup vinegar, 1 tablespoon olive oil and crushed rosemary. Cool to room temperature.

*I*n a small bowl, whisk together the olive oil, vinegar, mustard, garlic, salt and pepper.

*W*hen potatoes have cooled, add the mortadella squares, cheese strips, onion, parsley, capers and 1/2 cup dressing. Mix thoroughly, cover with plastic wrap and refrigerate for several hours. At serving time, transfer to an attractive salad bowl or platter, garnish with arugula leaves or lettuce, and drizzle with some of the remaining dressing.

*S*erves 6.

# European-Style Knackwurst Salad

*This type of salad is frequently found in the charcuteries of European cities. Add a basket of thick-sliced dark bread and cold beer for a hearty luncheon.*

5 knackwurst

1 cup thinly sliced celery

1 large onion, quartered and thinly sliced

1/2 cup chopped dill pickle

1/4 cup minced parsley

1 teaspoon tarragon, crushed

3/4 cup mayonnaise

2 tablespoons pickle juice

1 tablespoon Dijon-style mustard

3 hard-cooked eggs, chopped, for garnish

2 tablespoons minced parsley, for garnish

Simmer the knackwurst for 20 minutes, drain and cool slightly, then peel and slice thinly. When cooled to room temperature, add onions, celery, pickle, parsley and tarragon.

Mix together the mayonnaise, pickle juice and mustard and mix into the salad mixture. Mound in a bowl and garnish with the chopped eggs and minced parsley.

Serves 6.

# Lamb and Vegetable Salad

*A*n excellent way to use up leftover roast lamb is this flavorful
"salad-stew."

3 cups cooked lamb roast, cubed or
shredded

3 medium potatoes, cooked, quartered and
thinly sliced

3 carrots, thinly sliced and cooked until
barely tender

1 cup tiny frozen peas, thawed and blanched
with boiling water

1/2 cup diced dill pickle

1/2 cup crumbled feta cheese

1/2 cup olive oil

1/4 cup lemon juice

2 tablespoons mayonnaise

2 teaspoons Dijon-style mustard

1 tablespoon minced fresh dillweed or 1
teaspoon dried

1 garlic clove, minced

1/2 teaspoon salt, or more to taste

1/4 teaspoon freshly ground pepper

Boston or bibb lettuce leaves, to line bowl

2 tomatoes, sliced, for garnish

2 tablespoons minced parsley

1 tablespoons minced fresh dillweed

1 teaspoon grated lemon peel

*I*n a large bowl, combine the lamb, potatoes, carrots, peas, dill
pickles and feta cheese. Mix in 3/4 cup dressing, cover and marinate
for 2 hours at room temperature. Or prepare early in the day and
refrigerate. Bring to room temperature, taste for seasoning and mix
with remaining dressing before serving.

*L*ine a large salad bowl with lettuce leaves and add the salad. Garnish
with tomato slices; mix the parsley, dill and lemon peel and sprinkle
over the salad.

*S*erves 6.

# Middle Eastern Barley
# and Lamb Salad

*S*erve this salad with Herbed Pita Triangles; it would also make an interesting filling for pita bread sandwiches.

4 cups hot, cooked barley

2 cups roast lamb slivers

1 large cucumber, peeled, seeded and sliced

1/2 cup thinly sliced radishes

1/2 cup chopped green onions

1/2 cup chopped parsley

1/4 cup minced fresh mint (omit if fresh mint is unavailable)

1 cup olive oil

1/3 cup fresh lemon juice

1 teaspoon rosemary, crushed

1 garlic clove, minced

1 teaspoon salt

1/2 teaspoon freshly ground pepper

Shredded Boston lettuce and fresh spinach leaves to line salad plates

*I*n a small bowl, whisk together the oil, lemon juice, rosemary, garlic, salt and pepper.

*P*ut the hot, cooked barley in a large bowl and add 2/3 cup dressing; mix thoroughly and cool to room temperature. Add to the bowl the lamb, cucumber, radishes, green onions, parsley, mint and the remaining dressing. Taste for seasoning and adjust if necessary.

*A*rrange shredded lettuce and spinach on a large platter. Mound the salad in the center and serve.

*S*erves 6.

# Salad Con Carne with Taco Chips

*This salad has been a family favorite for years, long before the current "taco salad" craze. Serve with your favorite Mexican beer, guacamole and additional chips.*

1-1/2 pounds ground beef

1/2 cup coarsely chopped onion

1 large garlic clove, minced

8-ounce can tomato sauce

1.25-ounce package taco mix

1 teaspoon salt

1/4 teaspoon Tabasco sauce, or more to taste

1 head iceberg lettuce, cored and sliced 1-inch thick

2 medium tomatoes, cut in wedges

1 small red onion, thinly sliced and separated into rings

1 small green or red sweet pepper, thinly sliced

1/2 cup small ripe olives

1-1/2 cups shredded Cheddar cheese

6-ounce bag taco chips, coarsely crushed

*I*n a large skillet brown ground beef, onion and garlic. Spoon off as much fat as possible, mix in tomato sauce, taco mix, salt and Tabasco sauce; simmer about 10 minutes. Taste for seasoning and adjust if necessary. Keep meat warm while preparing salad bowl.

*I*n a large shallow bowl, toss lettuce, tomatoes, onion rings, pepper, olives and cheese. Spoon meat on salad and top with crushed chips. Serve immediately.

Serves 6.

# Picture Perfect Steak Salad

*This salad is as pleasing to look at as it is delicious to eat. Accompany with a basket of assorted breads and rolls.*

1-1/2 pounds flank steak brushed with olive oil and teriyaki sauce

1/2 pound green beans, trimmed and cut in 2-inch lengths

1 small red onion, thinly sliced and separated into rings

4 medium red potatoes, scrubbed, boiled and thinly sliced

1/4 cup hot beef broth

1/4 cup chopped green onions

1 garlic clove, minced

1/2 teaspoon rosemary, crushed

1 cup extra-virgin olive oil

1/3 cup red wine vinegar

2 tablespoons Dijon-style mustard

1 teaspoon salt

1/4 teaspoon freshly ground pepper

Red lettuce leaves, to line platter

Chopped parsley, for garnish

Grill or broil flank steak a total of 8 minutes. Cool, wrap tightly and refrigerate while preparing salad.

In a small bowl, whisk together oil, vinegar, mustard, salt and pepper.

Cook beans in boiling salted water about 5 minutes, or until just tender-crisp. Drain and run under cold water to stop cooking. Pat dry and mix with 1/4 cup dressing. Cool to room temperature.

Combine warm potato slices with beef broth, onions, garlic and rosemary; toss until broth has been absorbed. Add 1/2 cup dressing and mix to coat slices. Cool to room temperature. Prior to assembling the salad, slice the steak thinly across the grain, holding the knife at a 45 degree angle.

Line a large platter with lettuce leaves, arrange potato slices around the outer edge, cover with onion rings, layer green beans in the center and cover with steak slices. Drizzle 2 tablespoons of dressing over steak and sprinkle chopped parsley over salad. Serve immediately and pass remaining dressing separately.

Serves 6.

# Roast Beef, Olive and Nut Salad

*An unusual combination that is really very tasty.*

4 cups strips of cooked beef
1 cup halved pimento olives
Olive juice to thin mayonnaise
1 cup toasted pecans, coarsely chopped
1/4 cup chopped parsley
2/3 cup mayonnaise
1/2 teaspoon thyme
1/4 teaspoon freshly ground pepper
Salt to taste
Boston or bibb lettuce, to line bowl
4 hard-cooked eggs, sliced, for garnish
Pimento strips, for garnish

*In* a small bowl, mix mayonnaise with olive juice, pepper and salt, if needed.

*In* a bowl, mix together beef strips, olives, pecans, parsley and dressing. Cover and chill several hours.

*Line* a salad bowl with lettuce leaves, spoon salad in center and garnish with egg slices and pimento.

*Serves* 6.

# Cantonese Beef Salad with Green Peppers and Grapes

*This* salad has so many wonderful taste sensations, it's worth cooking a beef roast just to make the salad. Serve with a large bowl of crisp won ton strips.

4 cups cooked beef strips

2 sweet green peppers, cut into 1-inch pieces

1 heaping cup seedless green grapes

24 thin slices peeled ginger root

1 teaspoon salt

1 tablespoon white wine vinegar

2 teaspoons sugar

3 tablespoons soy sauce

2 tablespoons Chinese sesame paste (do not use tahini), available at Oriental grocery stores and some large supermarkets

1 tablespoon white wine vinegar

1 tablespoon catsup

1 teaspoon sesame oil

1 teaspoon sugar

Salt to taste

*In* a small bowl, mix ginger root with salt and let stand for 1 hour. Pour off any liquid and toss ginger slices with vinegar and sugar. Let stand for 2 hours before adding to salad.

*Blanch* pepper pieces in boiling water for 1 minute, drain, rinse with cold water and drain thoroughly.

*In* a large salad bowl, whisk together soy sauce, sesame paste, vinegar, catsup, oil and sugar. Add beef strips, pepper, grapes and ginger root and toss to coat with dressing. Taste for salt and other seasonings and adjust if necessary. Cover and chill lightly before serving.

*Serves* 6.

# Steak Salad with Cornichons and Anchovies

*A pricey steak will go a long way with this elegant and simple-to-prepare salad. Add a loaf of Easy Cheddar Braid and a glass of wine for a smashing luncheon.*

2 1/2 pound rib eye steaks, trimmed of fat and gristle

Olive oil for searing steaks

1/2 cup extra-virgin olive oil

1/3 cup red wine vinegar

1/2 cup minced parsley

4 green onions, minced

1/4 cup minced cornichons (available at specialty food stores and large supermarkets)

2-ounce tin anchovy fillets, drained and minced

1 tablespoon capers, drained

2 garlic cloves, minced

1/2 teaspoon rosemary, crushed

1/4 teaspoon freshly ground pepper

Salt to taste

Romaine lettuce and iceberg lettuce, thinly sliced, to line salad or dinner plates

12 cornichons, thinly sliced lengthwise almost to stem end and fanned out, for garnish

Watercress or parsley sprigs, for garnish

*I*n a large bowl, whisk together oil, vinegar, parsley, onions, cornichons, anchovies, capers, garlic, rosemary, pepper and salt to taste.

*I*n a large skillet, heat oil almost to smoking, add steaks and quickly sear on both sides so that meat will be medium-rare. Remove to a cutting board and cool about 10 minutes. Slice into 1/2-inch wide strips and add to bowl with dressing. Toss to coat, taste for seasoning and adjust if necessary. Immediately divide steak salad among 6 lettuce-lined plates, garnish with cornichons and watercress sprigs and serve.

*S*erves 6.

# Flank Steak, Snow Pea and Bean Sprout Salad

*To keep the Oriental theme going, start with Hot and Sour Soup and end with Mandarin orange slices tossed with powdered sugar and orange liqueur.*

2 pounds flank steak, brushed with olive oil and soy sauce

1/4 pound snow peas, tipped and strings removed

1/2 pound bean sprouts, rinsed under cold water and drained

1 sweet red pepper, julienned

1/2 cup chopped watercress leaves

1/4 cup white wine vinegar

3 tablespoons soy sauce

3 tablespoons salad oil

1 tablespoon sesame oil

1 teaspoon grated ginger root

1/4 teaspoon crushed red pepper flakes

Salt to taste

1 tablespoon toasted sesame seeds, for garnish

Watercress sprigs, for garnish

Blanch snow peas in boiling salted water for 30 seconds; drain, rinse with cold water, drain thoroughly and pat dry.

In a large serving bowl, whisk together vinegar, soy sauce, salad oil, sesame oil, ginger root, pepper flakes and salt to taste.

Broil the steak in a preheated broiler, about 2 inches from the heat, for a total of 6 minutes. Remove to a cutting board and let rest for about 10 minutes. Holding the knife at a 45-degree angle, slice the meat into 1/4-inch thick slices. Add meat and any accumulated juices to the bowl, and toss with the dressing. Add snow peas, bean sprouts, pepper and watercress leaves and mix gently. Sprinkle with sesame seeds and garnish with watercress sprigs. Serve immediately.

Serves 6.

# Beef, Lentil and Spinach Salad

*Next time you plan to serve flank steak, prepare an extra one to use for this unique salad.*

1 pound flank steak, rubbed with a garlic clove and brushed with olive oil

1-1/2 cups lentils, picked over and rinsed

12-ounce package fresh spinach, thoroughly rinsed, tough stems removed and coarsely chopped

1/2 cup thinly sliced green onions

3/4 cup olive oil

1/4 cup vinegar

1 tablespoon horseradish

2 garlic cloves, minced

1 teaspoon thyme

1/2 teaspoon salt, or more to taste

1/4 teaspoon freshly ground pepper

Chopped parsley, for garnish

*B*roil the steak about 2 inches from the heat source for a total of 6 minutes. Remove to a board and cool before slicing across the grain into 1/4-inch wide strips.

*A*dd lentils to 6 cups salted water, bring to a boil, reduce heat and simmer about 20 minutes or until barely tender. Drain in a colander and cool to room temperature.

*I*n a large bowl, whisk together oil, vinegar, horseradish, garlic, thyme, salt and pepper. Add steak, lentils and onions and mix thoroughly. Taste for seasonings and adjust if necessary. Serve at room temperature or lightly chilled. Garnish with parsley before serving.

*S*erves 6.

# Sizzling Steak and Avocado Salad

*Y*ou *might like to precede this salad with a cup of cold consomme garnished with julienned carrots and sweet red peppers. Serve both with Peppery Cheese Biscuits.*

2 pounds beef tenderloin, cut into 1-inch cubes

Seasoned salt and freshly ground pepper

3 avocados, sliced and sprinkled with lemon juice to prevent tarnishing

2 large Belgian endives, trimmed and sliced crosswise into 1/2-inch slices

Watercress sprigs

Boston lettuce, to line serving plates

2/3 cup mayonnaise

1/2 cup cooked frozen chopped spinach, well drained

1/3 cup pickle relish

2 tablespoons white wine

2 teaspoons lemon juice

1/2 teaspoon dry mustard

1/2 teaspoon sugar

1/2 teaspoon salt, or more to taste

*I*n a small bowl, mix together mayonnaise, spinach, relish, wine, lemon juice, dry mustard, sugar and salt. Adjust seasonings if necessary.

*L*ine 6 dinner plates with whole lettuce leaves; arrange avocado, endive and watercress around outer edges of lettuce.

*A*rrange steak cubes on an oiled broiler rack, broil about 2 inches from heat source for 2 minutes. Turn with tongs and broil 1 minute. Remove to a bowl and sprinkle with seasoned salt and freshly ground pepper. With a slotted spoon, transfer steak cubes to salad plates. Mix any remaining meat juice into dressing and spoon a few dollops onto each salad. Pass remaining dressing separately.

*S*erves 6.

# Corned Beef Salad

*If you have a yearning for corned beef salad but leftovers aren't available, ask the deli-person to slice the deli corned beef extra thick so you can cut that into cubes.*

3 cups cooked corned beef, cubed or shredded

1 cup chopped dill pickles

1/2 cup thinly sliced celery

1/2 cup chopped sweet red or green pepper

1/2 cup chopped green onions

3/4 cup mayonnaise

2 tablespoons dill pickle juice

1 tablespoon minced fresh dillweed, or 1 teaspoon dried

1/2 teaspoon salt

1/4 teaspoon freshly ground pepper

Lettuce leaves, to line salad bowl

4 hard-cooked eggs, sliced, for garnish

Pimento olives, for garnish

*In* a large bowl, mix together corned beef, pickles, celery, pepper and onions.

*In* a small bowl, mix together mayonnaise, pickle juice, dillweed, salt and pepper. Pour dressing over salad and mix. Cover and chill for several hours or overnight.

*To* serve, line a large bowl with lettuce, spoon salad in the center, ring with egg slices and garnish with olives.

*Serves 6.*

# How to Cook Beef Tongue

3-1/2 to 4 pound smoked or pickled beef
tongue

1 carrot, scraped and cut in 2-inch lengths

1 stalk celery, with leaves, quartered

1 small onion

2 tablespoons pickling spice

*P*lace tongue, vegetables and spices in a large pot; add cold water to
cover tongue. Cover and bring to a boil, reduce heat and simmer,
partially covered, 2-1/2 hours. Cool the tongue in the water, transfer
to a cutting board and remove fat and gristle from the large end of the
tongue. Wrap in foil or plastic wrap and refrigerate several hours or
overnight before slicing.

# Tongue Salad Les Halles

*This is a classic salad found in the bistros and charcuteries of Paris. Of course, a baguette of French bread is the classic accompaniment.*

2 pounds pickled or smoked tongue, preferably home-cooked (see page 150)

1 cup coarsely chopped red onion

1/2 cup extra-virgin olive oil

1/3 cup white wine or herb vinegar

1 teaspoon sugar

1/2 teaspoon thyme

1/2 teaspoon salt

1/4 teaspoon freshly ground pepper

2 whole bay leaves

Boston or bibb lettuce, to line platter

18 cornichons (available in gourmet food stores and some large supermarkets), for garnish

Slice tongue 1/3-inch thick, then cut slices into 1/2-inch wide strips. Combine in a glass or ceramic bowl with the onions.

In a small saucepan, bring to a boil the oil, vinegar, sugar, thyme, salt, pepper and bay leaves. Reduce heat and simmer about 3 minutes. Pour dressing over the tongue and onions, cool and refrigerate overnight. Bring the salad to room temperature and remove bay leaves before serving.

To serve, line a shallow bowl with lettuce leaves, spoon salad in the center and garnish with cornichons.

Serves 6.

# Tongue, Potato and Spinach Salad

*For some reason, this salad makes us think of Ireland. Try it with soda bread and cold beer.*

2 pounds smoked tongue, cut into 1/3-inch slices, then into 1-inch strips (see page 150)

4 medium potatoes, boiled, peeled and diced

1/2 cup thinly sliced celery

1/2 cup chopped sweet red or green pepper

1/2 cup chopped green onions

2 tablespoons capers, drained

12-ounce bag fresh spinach, well rinsed, tough stems removed and patted dry

2/3 cup extra-virgin olive oil

3 tablespoons red wine vinegar

3 tablespoons mayonnaise

1 tablespoon Dijon-style mustard

1 tablespoon minced fresh dillweed or 1 teaspoon dried

1/2 teaspoon sugar

1/2 teaspoon salt

1/4 teaspoon freshly ground pepper

2 hard-cooked eggs, chopped, for garnish

Minced parsley, for garnish

*I*n a small bowl, whisk together oil, vinegar, mayonnaise, mustard, dillweed, sugar, salt and pepper.

*I*n a large bowl, mix together tongue, potatoes, celery, pepper, onions, capers and 1/2 cup dressing. Taste for seasoning and adjust if necessary. Cover and chill for several hours or overnight.

*T*o serve, toss rinsed and dried spinach with 1/4 cup dressing and arrange around the outer edge of a platter. Mound tongue salad in the center, sprinkle the spinach with chopped eggs and garnish the salad with parsley. Pass any remaining dressing separately.

Serves 6.

# Tongue Salad

*This is a nice alternative to the usual ham salad. Serve with a basket of thick-sliced dark bread or Caraway Biscuits.*

2 pounds smoked tongue, preferably home-cooked (see page 150)

1 cup thinly sliced celery

1/2 cup thinly sliced sweet gherkins

1/4 cup chopped onions

1/4 cup chopped parsley

2/3 cup mayonnaise

1 tablespoon Dijon-style mustard

1 tablespoon gherkin pickle juice

1/4 teaspoon freshly ground pepper

Salt to taste

Romaine lettuce, to line salad bowl

6 hard-cooked eggs, halved

Ask the deli-person to slice the tongue 1/3-inch thick. Julienne the slices into 1/2-inch strips. In a large bowl, mix tongue, celery, gherkins, onions and parsley.

In a small bowl, mix together mayonnaise, mustard, pickle juice, pepper and salt to taste. Add just enough dressing to salad to bind it together. Cover and refrigerate overnight or for several hours. Before serving, mix salad and add more dressing as needed.

To serve, line a bowl with lettuce leaves, spoon salad in center, and surround with egg halves.

Serves 6.

# Tongue and Chicken Salad Loaf

*This* salad takes more care in preparing so you might want to save it for a special occasion. Polish up that silver tray to present it on.

1-1/2 cups cooked smoked tongue, diced
6 thin slices of tongue
3/4 cup cooked chicken, diced
3/4 cup thinly sliced celery
1 egg, lightly beaten
1/4 cup white wine vinegar
1 teaspoon prepared mustard
1/2 teaspoon sugar
2 teaspoons butter
1/3 cup mayonnaise

1/4 cup minced parsley
1 tablespoon minced onion
Salt and pepper to taste
2 packages plain gelatin
2 tablespoons cold water
1 cup beef broth
1 tablespoon lemon juice
1 teaspoon Worcestershire sauce
3 tablespoons minced parsley
Shredded mixed greens, to line platter

*I*n a small saucepan, over low heat, cook egg, vinegar, mustard, and sugar until it thickens to the consistency of mayonnaise. Remove from the heat and stir in the butter. Transfer to a large bowl to cool, then add diced tongue, diced chicken, celery, mayonnaise, parsley, onion, salt and pepper to taste.

*I*n a small bowl, soften gelatin in cold water for 10 minutes.

*I*n a small saucepan, combine beef broth, lemon juice and Worcestershire sauce; bring to a boil and stir in gelatin. Remove from the heat and stir in the parsley. Cool the mixture but do not let it set.

*L*ightly oil a 9 x 5 loaf pan and pour in about 1/4-inch aspic mixture. Dip the tongue slices into the saucepan of aspic, then line the bottom and sides of the pan. Chill about 15 minutes, until set.

*S*tir the remaining aspic into the diced tongue and chicken mixture and spoon into the loaf pan. Rap the pan sharply on the countertop to remove any air spaces. Cover and chill the loaf overnight.

*B*efore serving, run a knife around the edge of the loaf pan, invert on an appropriate platter. Trim with the washed and dried salad greens. Slice and serve with the greens.

*S*erves 6.

# Accompaniments

# Accompaniments

*T*his chapter contains some favorite recipes for bread and crackers to accompany these hearty salads. All are fast and easy to make, and always add an extra-special and appreciated note.

# Anchovy Toasts

2-ounce tin anchovy fillets, drained and
coarsely chopped

1 teaspoon capers, drained

1 tablespoon lemon juice

1/4 teaspoon freshly ground pepper, or more
to taste

1/2 cup extra-virgin olive oil, divided

12 1/2-inch slices French bread

Add to a food processor bowl or blender jar anchovies, capers,
lemon juice, pepper and 1/4 cup oil; blend until a smooth paste forms.
Scrape into a small bowl and set aside until ready to use.

Brush both sides of French bread with remaining oil; toast both sides
in a toaster-oven or under a broiler, about 4 inches from the heat,
until golden on both sides. Spread with the anchovy paste and return
to the broiler or "top brown" setting of a toaster-oven, until bubbly
and puffed.

To prepare ahead, spread toasted slices with anchovy spread, place
on a cookie sheet or plate, cover with plastic wrap and refrigerate
until serving time.

Yields 12 pieces.

# Caraway Biscuits

2/3 cup flour

1/3 cup whole wheat flour

2 tablespoons wheat germ

1-1/2 teaspoons baking powder

1/2 teaspoon salt

1/4 cup butter or margarine, at room temperature

1 teaspoon caraway seeds, lightly crushed if possible

1/3 cup milk, or more if necessary

1-2 tablespoons melted butter to brush on biscuit tops

*P*reheat oven to 450 degrees; lightly grease baking sheet.

*C*ombine in a food processor bowl or mixing bowl flour, whole wheat flour, wheat germ, baking powder and salt. Cut in butter until mixture forms coarse crumb-like texture. Add caraway seeds and milk and blend just until a firm, but not stiff, dough forms. Turn out onto a floured pastry cloth or other surface, and pat into a 1/2-inch thick rectangle. Fold top third over middle third and bring bottom third up over this. Roll out into a 1/2-inch-thick circle. With a biscuit cutter or the rim of a glass, cut 12 biscuits. Place on the baking sheet, brush with melted butter and bake 15 to 20 minutes. Biscuits can be frozen and reheated in a microwave or conventional oven until heated through. Do not thaw before reheating; cover lightly with paper towel (microwave oven) or foil (conventional oven) to prevent drying.

*Y*ields 12 biscuits.

# Dann's Beer Biscuits

4 cups biscuit mix

2 tablespoons sugar

1/2 teaspoon celery seed, or dried herb of
your choice

1 can light beer, cold and newly opened

*P*reheat oven to 350 degrees. Either line muffin tins with paper liners or lightly grease.

*I*n a bowl, mix together biscuit mix, sugar, celery seed or herbs and beer. Spoon into 16-18 muffin cups, bake about 20 minutes, or until lightly browned on top. Muffins can be frozen. Do not thaw before reheating. Cover lightly with paper towel (microwave oven) or foil (conventional oven) to prevent drying out.

*Y*ields 16-18 muffins.

# Dann's Beer Bread

3 cups self-rising flour
2 tablespoons sugar
1 teaspoon dillweed, or herb of your choice
1 can beer, cold and newly opened

*P*reheat oven to 350 degrees; lightly grease a 9 x 5 inch loaf pan.

*I*n a bowl, mix together flour, sugar, dill or herb and beer. Spoon into prepared pan and bake about 50-60 minutes, until top is nicely browned and loaf sounds hollow when tapped on the top.

*Y*ields 1 loaf.

# Easy Cheddar Braid

16-ounce package white yeast-bread mix

2 cups grated sharp Cheddar cheese

1/2 teaspoon crushed red pepper flakes
(subtitute 1/2 teaspoon basil if red pepper
does not appeal to you)

1 egg, lightly beaten, divided

2 tablespoons grated Parmesan cheese

Preheat oven to 375 degrees; lightly grease a baking sheet.

Follow package directions for preparing dough but omit oil and stir Cheddar cheese, pepper flakes and 1 tablespoon beaten egg into flour-yeast mixture. After the 5-minute rest period, cut dough into thirds. On a floured pastry cloth or other surface, roll each piece into a 14-inch long rope. Place each rope side by side on the greased baking sheet. Start braiding ropes from the middle to one end. Flip dough over and repeat braiding to the other end. Pinch ends together to seal. Cover and let rise in a warm place about 15 minutes.

Brush with remaining egg and sprinkle with Parmesan cheese. Bake on the center rack of preheated oven about 30 minutes or until lightly browned and loaf sounds hollow when tapped. Remove to rack and cool before slicing. Bread can be frozen. To reheat, wrap, frozen, in foil and heat in a 350-degree oven 15-20 minutes.

Yields about 14 slices.

# *Parsley Skillet Bread*

3 cups flour

1-1/2 teaspoons baking powder

1 teaspoon freshly ground pepper

1/2 teaspoon salt

3/4 cup minced parsley

1/2 cup well-chilled butter or margarine, cut
into 10 pieces

1 cup half-and-half

1 teaspoon olive oil

Freshly ground pepper

*P*reheat oven to 425 degrees. Generously butter a 9-inch iron skillet or a 9-inch glass pie plate.

*I*n the bowl of a food processor, blend flour, baking powder, pepper and salt. Add parsley and process with a few on/off pulses. Cut in butter just until mixture has a coarse-crumb texture. With the motor running, slowly add the cream through the feed tube and mix just until a ball forms. Turn out onto a floured pastry cloth or other surface, and pat into a 9-inch flat round. Transfer dough to skillet or pie plate. Brush with oil and sprinkle with pepper. Bake about 30 minutes or until light brown and crisp around the edges. Remove to a rack and cool before slicing into wedges.

*Y*ields 8 wedges.

# Cheese and Chili Pepper Biscuits

2/3 cup freshly grated Fontina cheese

2 cups flour

1 tablespoon baking powder

1/2 teaspoon baking soda

1/2 teaspoon salt

1/4 cup butter or margarine, cut into 6 pieces

2 tablespoons canned, chopped chili peppers, well drained

1 cup buttermilk or 1 cup milk mixed with 1 tablespoon vinegar or lemon juice

2 tablespoons melted butter

*P*reheat oven to 450 degrees; lightly grease a baking sheet.

*I*n the bowl of a food processor combine with a couple of on/off pulses cheese, flour, baking powder, baking soda and salt. Cut in butter pieces with repeated pulses until mixture is the texture of coarse crumbs. Add the chili peppers to the bowl. With the motor running, slowly add the buttermilk through the feed tube and mix just until dough gathers together. Turn out onto a floured pastry cloth or other surface, and with floured hands knead 10 or 12 times. Roll dough into a 12-inch flat round and cut with a 1-1/2-inch mini-biscuit cutter, or a 2-1/2-inch cutter if preferred. Place biscuits about 1 inch apart on the greased baking sheet, brush tops with melted butter and bake in preheated oven about 10 minutes or until lightly browned. Biscuits can be frozen. Reheat, unthawed, wrapped in foil in a preheated 350 degree oven about 15 minutes.

*Y*ields about 24 small or 16 larger biscuits.

# Herbed Pita Triangles

4 large pita loaves

1/2 cup softened butter or margarine

2 tablespoons minced parsley

1 tablespoon lemon juice

1 large garlic clove, minced

1/2 teaspoon each thyme, basil and oregano

1/4 teaspoon salt, or more to taste

Slice pita loaves horizontally; cut each half into 4 or 8 pieces, depending on how large you prefer the wedges.

In a small bowl, mix together butter, parsley, lemon juice, garlic, herbs and salt. Spread the inside of each triangle with butter mixture, arrange pita on a baking sheet, cover with plastic wrap and refrigerate until ready to heat. Or wrap tightly in foil and freeze. Do not thaw before baking.

Preheat oven to 400 degrees; bake triangles for 5 minutes or until slightly crisp and brown.

Yields 16 large or 32 small triangles.

# Jiffy Oat and Raisin Bread

1-1/4 cup flour

1 cup regular or quick-cooking oat flakes (do not use instant)

1/2 cup raisins

1 tablespoon sugar

1-1/2 teaspoons baking powder

1/2 teaspoon baking soda

1/2 teaspoon ground cardamom

1/4 teaspoon salt

1 cup buttermilk or 1 cup milk mixed with 1 tablespoon lemon juice or vinegar

1/4 cup melted butter or margarine

1 egg

1 teaspoon grated lemon or orange peel

*P*reheat oven to 425 degrees; lightly grease a 9-inch round baking pan.

*I*n a large bowl, mix together flour, oats, sugar, baking powder, baking soda and salt. In a small bowl, mix together buttermilk, butter, egg and lemon or orange peel. Add to the dry ingredients and mix with a wooden spoon just until combined. Pour into greased pan and bake 15 minutes; reduce heat to 350 degrees and bake about 25 minutes or until bread starts to pull away from pan and center is dry when a toothpick is inserted. Cool in the pan for 10 minutes. Turn out onto a round plate, cut into wedges and serve. Bread can be tightly wrapped in foil after it is completely cool and frozen. Thaw about 1 hour, then reheat in a 325-degree oven about 20 minutes; keep lightly wrapped in foil.

*Y*ield one 9-inch loaf.

# Garlicky-Cheesy French Bread

1 French baguette
2 cups grated Swiss cheese
3 garlic cloves, minced
2 tablespoons minced parsley
1 teaspoon thyme
1/2 teaspoon salt
1/4 cup milk

Preheat oven to 400 degrees. Cut bread in diagonal slices, not quite all the way through, 1-1/2-inches wide.

Mix together in a bowl cheese, garlic, parsley, thyme, salt and milk. Spread or pat a spoonful of mixture between each slice. Wrap baguette tightly in foil and bake about 15 minutes, or just until cheese starts to melt.

Yields about 18 slices, depending on length of bread.

Maxine Rapoport and Nina Graybill are co-authors of THE PASTA SALAD BOOK, COLD SOUPS, and ENJOY! MAKE-AHEAD DINNER PARTY MENUS. They live in Washington, D.C. For many years, Ms. Rapoport has pursued a wide range of culinary interests, not the least of which is delighting family and friends with her gift for cooking. Ms. Graybill, a literary lawyer, cooks dinner and writes cookbooks whenever she finds the time.